Claude Reignier Conder

The Bible and the East

Claude Reignier Conder

The Bible and the East

ISBN/EAN: 9783743385740

Manufactured in Europe, USA, Canada, Australia, Japa

Cover: Foto ©Lupo / pixelio.de

Manufactured and distributed by brebook publishing software (www.brebook.com)

Claude Reignier Conder

The Bible and the East

THE BIBLE AND THE EAST

BY

C. R. CONDER, Lt.-Col. R.E.

LL.D., D.C.L., M.R.A.S.

WILLIAM BLACKWOOD AND SONS
EDINBURGH AND LONDON
MDCCCXCVI

CONTENTS.

CHAP.		PAGE
	INTRODUCTION	1
I.	IN THE BEGINNING	5
II.	THE PATRIARCHS	19
III.	THE EXODUS	35
IV.	HEBREW CIVILISATION	53
V.	THE PENTATEUCH	79
VI.	JOSHUA	101
VII.	JUDGES	117
VIII.	SAMUEL AND DAVID	127
IX.	KINGS	143
X.	THE PROPHETS	165
XI.	HEBREW POETRY	173
XII.	THE PERSIAN AGE	193
XIII.	DANIEL	201
XIV.	THE TIME OF CHRIST	207
	INDEX	231

LIST OF ILLUSTRATIONS.

STATUE OF JUDEA	*Frontispiece*
(After De Sarzek.)	
	PAGE
HITTITES FROM ABU SIMBEL	21
(Author's Sketch, lent by Messrs George Philip & Son.)	
MOABITE STONE	54
(From Photo lent by Palestine Exploration Fund.)	
COMPARATIVE PLATE OF ALPHABETS	63
(Lent by Palestine Exploration Fund.)	
HAMATH STONE, NO. 1	75
(Author's Sketch, lent by Messrs George Philip & Son.)	
LACHISH TABLET	104, 105
(Author's Copy, lent by Palestine Exploration Fund.)	
SILOAM INSCRIPTION	156
(Author's Copy, lent by Palestine Exploration Fund.)	
PALACE OF HYRCANUS	209
(Author's Sketch, lent by Palestine Exploration Fund.)	
INSCRIPTION OF HEROD'S TEMPLE	212
(From Photo lent by Palestine Exploration Fund.)	
MAP OF PALESTINE	*At end*

THE BIBLE AND THE EAST.

INTRODUCTION.

NEVER was the Bible more read or more earnestly studied than now; for—imperfect though they be—the means of understanding it daily become more and better. The same spirit of freedom and love of truth which led to its being rendered in the vulgar tongue, lead us still to claim to read and study its pages without limits set to the right of private judgment. They are viewed from many standpoints by the student of natural science, of literature, or of antiquities. These great departments of knowledge have been pursued for their own sake, and by men who cared little as a rule for other sciences; and they have led to various conclusions which often are at discord. To understand the Bible aright, all of these must be taken into account. But if private judgment has taken the place of authority in the study of the Bible, this is not less true of the study of science. No dicta of even the greatest are to be accepted, unless the reasoning on which they are founded proves to be sound. With improved data we find such conclusions to be constantly liable to change—in science, literature, and archæology alike. The results of criticism have not always stood the test of examination in the light of monumental discovery; and history once discarded as fabulous has often proved to record actual facts. Contradictions which seemed clear have been shown to be due to a false assumption on the part of the student, and prejudice discovered where impartial judgment was claimed.

Within the present century we have witnessed not only the recovery of unhoped-for sources of knowledge, and the growth of sciences founded on painful gathering of unknown facts, but revolutions not less remarkable in the principles on which studies of every kind are founded. Comparative examination of independent facts is now the basis of all true knowledge, and the comparison grows ever wider. The slow growth of the future from the past is accepted as explaining all that has happened in our world, and the decay of all that once flourished is not less to be remembered in tracing history aright.

In natural science the belief in a slow development of life on the planet, and in the great antiquity of man—historically speaking—is generally accepted. In literature the minute examination of language and historic statement has undermined many traditional beliefs. In the study of antiquity the early civilisation of Asia has been proved to have been more perfect, and more widely spread, than scholars were willing once to believe. All these changes have affected our study of the Bible, and will yet more affect it in the future. But the Bible needs no apology, and its words are as deeply rooted in men's hearts to-day as ever they were in times of greater ignorance. Neither science, literature, nor oriental study can touch—or aim at touching—the teaching of love and truth in its pages. The study of other Sacred Books of the East only serves to show us the greatness of the Bible compared with other books. It is only the timid who fear the light poured on the Hebrew Scriptures by modern science or discovery; for while the honest student may be forced to give up much that he once believed, to own that tradition among Hebrew writers in time, as in other cases, sometimes overlaid the figures of great heroes with popular legend, and that they speak to us in the tongue of their own age, not in the language of to-day,—yet the honesty, the power, the genius, and the inspiration of prophets and psalmists in Israel are the more truly acknowledged the more freely their scrolls are studied and their statements examined.

It is a question how best to approach so wide a subject, and what sequence of studies to follow; but to conform roughly to the order of the books of the Old and New Testament, and to take in order the various questions of history, civilisation, literature, and religion in various ages, from the patriarchal to the Roman, seems the most easy method for the reader. The main object in view is to show the bearing of exploration and monumental study on the understanding of the Bible, and to such study natural science and criticism are secondary helps. No student of critical writings can doubt that services of the highest value have been rendered by scholars who have spent their lives on the various languages required, on comparison of versions, and on mastering the writings of those who went before. Yet such purely internal study has often led to conclusions which have been falsified by the recovery of a single monumental text. No Bible scholar can afford to neglect the teaching of such sciences as geology, natural history, or astronomy. Yet even in these, imperfect knowledge has created difficulties which fade away in the light of a better study. Our aim should be to read the Bible without bias in favour of Rabbinical tradition, but also without too hastily accepting the latest transient theory of any critic or writer on science.

CHAPTER I.

IN THE BEGINNING.

THE first chapter of Genesis no longer stands alone in literature as an ancient story of Creation. The brick tablets of Assyria contain more than one ancient poem on Creation; the Persian account, preserved in sacred writings of a late age, presents us with an almost exact copy of the Hebrew six days.[1] But in the one case the beauty of the story is marred by strange names for many gods, and the sequence is imperfect and the details tedious; while in the other the present version is of so late a date as to make it useless for comparison.[2]

> "At first God carved the heavens and earth,
> And earth was vast and void,
> And darkness on the face of the deep;
> And God's breath hovered on the waters' face,
> And God said, Be there light;
> And there was light . . .
> And eve and morn one day."

Neither in Assyrian tablets, in Greek cosmogonies, nor in later philosophies, does any ancient writer reach the sim-

---

[1] See Lenormant's Origines de l'Histoire, vol. i.
[2] Bundahish, Sacred Books of the East, vol. v.

plicity of such words. The clumsy systems of the past have died and left the Hebrew alone in face of modern science. The Bible story tells us of the gradual growth of earth itself, of land and sea, of herbs and trees; of the appearance of sun and moon and planets, the birth of fish and fowl and beast, and, at the last, of man in a world prepared for him—"male and female created He them."

The astronomy of to-day speaks of a red-hot orb thrown out from the sun, cooling gradually till land and sea were separated under the dense clouds which hid the planet; of creeping things and herbs, succeeded by the dense forests and marshes in which huge dragons waded and flew, while giant monsters peopled the deep. In the later birth of birds and beasts, and in the appearance of man—the latest of all—there is no real discrepancy between the results of natural science and the more primitive language of the Hebrew poet. It has been argued that the sun is said by him to have been made after the earth—yet on the very first day "eve and morn" are mentioned. No man of science doubts that, just as we are still unable to see the surface of one great planet through its thick garb of cloud, so on earth neither sun nor moon nor stars appeared until the mighty vapours were dissolved which once hid our planet also. The great forests of the coal measures grew rank in their swamps at a time when the sun's heat only reached them through the fog. The Hebrew writer may have believed, like his fellows, in a firmament of adamant and in a central earth; but the story of Creation as a whole is the story of an evolution.

How long ago it was that man first began to conquer the earth science cannot tell us surely. That at least 2700 years before our era there were in Asia various civilisations and distinct races, is the testimony of the monuments. That man in Europe lived in an early age when the mammoth and many other extinct beasts were yet alive,—that he even had learned to sketch them on bone before they became extinct,—is the testimony of the caves. Long ages must have elapsed before the art of writing in various scripts had attained to the stage it reached in Mesopotamia and Egypt five thousand years ago, or before the limestone flooring of the bone-caves had hardened over the remains of men and beasts. But as yet our knowledge of such ages is confined to diggings in European caves and river-drifts, and the history of man in his earliest home is unknown, and the age of his first appearance incalculable.

We may ask, however, with more hope of an answer, whether science and the Bible are agreed as to the first centre of the race, and as to the history of its dispersion over the earth. Science teaches us that early man passed through two stages of rough culture, using at first unshapen stones for weapons and tools, and then polishing the same—the palæolithic and neolithic stages—before he knew of copper, of bronze, and of iron last of all. Yet, curiously enough, these stages have been thought to mark successive ages, in spite of the fact that tribes still living in remote regions have never passed beyond the use of stone. Until about 600 B.C. the Europeans of the north knew nothing of the use of bronze, which had been commonly worked in Asia more than a thousand years before. The stone age in Egypt was immensely earlier than that of Britain; and most of the prehistoric relics of Europe—the Swiss lake-villages, the Guernsey dolmens, the tomb-mounds of our own country—belong to later times than those in which literature and art already flourished in Western Asia. To speak, therefore, of a "palæolithic age" is to ignore the facts of history. The "palæolithic stage" is by itself no mark of any measurable lapse of time.

Whatever the time, however, the verdict of science now is[1] that in the palæolithic period man appeared in Asia on open plains, in a temperate or subtropical region, where seeds, game, and fish abounded—to become first a hunter, then a herdsman, finally a tiller of the earth, as witnessed by the succession of palæolithic remains in Europe. This home was somewhere in the plateaux of Persia or farther east, and to such a centre the traditions of many early races point alike. The Greek looked to Caucasus, and the "Aryan home" of the Persians was in the same region. Indians and Chinese tribes had their sacred mountains in the far north-west and west. The early Akkadians came from the Kurdish valleys: the Hebrew writer points to the uplands of Eastern Armenia, and to the sources of the Tigris and Euphrates, where was that garden in the East whence man came forth to till the

[1] Wallace, Darwinism, p. 459. London, 1889.

earth. It is a region well fitted for the early home of man, with temperate climate and natural fruits of the earth, with great rivers and fertile valleys. From such a centre many nations spread on every side—the Aryan to the Volga, the Mongol over Asia, and the forefathers of Semitic races to Chaldea, Arabia, and Syria, preceded by the Egyptian, to whom they were akin.

The study of language is our only guide in this dim age of early migration,[1] but the evidence, such as it is, all points to one conclusion. It is admitted that a chain of dialects connects the most distant regions of the earth with early centres in Western Asia, where the first traces of various families of speech are found. The languages of Mongolia and China, the early speech of India, Burmah, and Siam, are all connected by words and grammar with the first Mongol dialects of Upper Chaldea. The great families of American languages belong to the same group, as do the dialects of Oceana and Australia peopled from the Siamese peninsula. The Aryan languages are traced to the earliest centre on the Volga, and on the steppes of Southern Russia. The languages of Africa show close connection with the ancient Egyptian, which again is linked with the Semitic group. Already it has been perceived that a connection exists between Mongolic and Aryan speech—a connection which may also be extended to the other groups which share a large common vocabulary of roots. Western Asia is not only the home of civilisation, but it is the region to which the various

[1] See note, p. 13.

families of human speech are traced—to a centre including homes of Mongol, Aryan, and Semitic races alike. Distinguished as they are by racial type,—the heavy short-headed Mongol, the fair Aryan, the dusky Semitic man, the coffee-coloured Egyptian, or the black Negro,—such types do not so differ as to make specific distinction. In the earliest graves of Asia and of Europe the long and short heads are found together as in Egypt, and some of the older are less pronounced in measurement than are later remains. The head of a Galla or of an Egyptian differs little from that of a European. The prognathous or protruding jaw is as marked in the more degraded type of the Mongol as in the degraded Negro type. On the equator alone is man really coal-black in colour. The Kaffir, the Polynesian, or the Dravidian in India, are scarcely darker than some of the Mongols and Arabs. In the fens of North Russia Aryan races are thought to have been bleached by ages of cold; and colour alone is not enough to establish various human species. The study of race and of language is still in its infancy; but no discovery of science forbids us to assume that man may originally have descended from a single human pair, living in Western Asia and speaking a language of the simplest elements, from which all human speech has been built up in time.

Yet another mark of common origin is found in common tradition, pointing, however, to a later time, since it is unknown in Egypt or in Africa.[1] The European,

[1] Lenormant, Origines de l'Histoire, vol. i. See note, p. 16.

the Asiatic, and the American have all in common the story of a Flood from which their ancestors escaped. The Assyrian account (about the seventh century B.C.) is nearest to the Hebrew, but forms part of a wild cycle of legends belonging to the twelve months of the year. The Greek may have taken it from the Phœnician. The Persian story substitutes a terrible winter escaped by Yima in his "enclosure," to which a bird (as in the Chaldean story) brings the first news of spring. But the Flood story was known also to the Celts in Europe—the earliest of Western Aryans—and to the Northern Indians and the Chinese. It has been found in America, and it was known apparently to the early Akkadian Mongols. Connected though it often is with legends of the months and the mythical story of the year, there is still no reason to deny that it may represent in every case the memory of some great catastrophe in early times, and of the escape of a few survivors in Asia. In earlier geologic times such catastrophes are witnessed by the piles of bones of beasts who perished on the uplands where they found refuge from the rising tide. The variations of the Flood story indicate rather a common memory, handed down by tradition, than any borrowing of a later finished tale. The widespread character of the tradition points to an age earlier than that of the dispersion of the various Asiatic races. The floods of the Tigris and of the Euphrates continued to be feared much later by the writers of Akkadian hymns and prayers, and the time of year—the middle of the second month mentioned in Genesis—is that in which the Tigris and the Euphrates are swelled by the melting snows of Armenia. Science forbids us to suppose that at any time since man's first appearance was the whole surface of the world submerged at one time, or that all existing species of living things were ever collected in an ark or boat; but the tradition of an early catastrophe, and of the escape of the few, was handed down in all parts of Europe and of Asia among races to whom the Hebrew Scriptures and the Assyrian tablets alike were never known.

NOTES TO CHAPTER I.

Comparison of Languages.—This subject will be found more fully treated in the author's paper, read before the Victoria Institute in 1893. The similarities between Aryan and Semitic roots were noticed by Gesenius before the scientific study of Aryan languages had been founded by Bopp and Grimm. The similarities of Aryan and Finnic roots have also been indicated by Donner and other scholars, and recently urged by Dr Isaac Taylor in his work on the Aryans. The relationship of Egyptian to Semitic speech was urged by the late Dr Birch of the British Museum. The main objections which have to be met are, first, the differences of grammatical structure distinguishing inflected languages (such as the Aryan and the Semitic) from agglutinative speech (such as marks the Mongol and American languages); and, secondly, the undoubted fact that a large vocabulary has often been borrowed by one class of languages from another. The principles on which comparative study of various classes of language must be founded include, first, the comparison of the roots from which words are formed rather than that of isolated nouns or verbs; and, secondly, the restriction of such comparisons to the earliest known languages. The Aryan languages have been reduced to certain recognised roots, of which the simplest category does not probably exceed about 150 in all. The Finnic languages are reduced by Donner to an equally small number of roots; and by Vambéry the Turkic dialects are similarly reduced to about 200 roots. The comparison of these categories at once shows the large proportion of roots common to Aryan and to Mongol speech; and in addition it can be shown that the Mongol vocabulary is comparable throughout with that of the ancient Mongol language of Mesopotamia, commonly called the Akkadian (see the paper by the present author in the 'Journal of the Royal Asiatic Society,' October 1893). The pure Turkish dialects of Central Asia appear to be nearest to the Akkadian, especially in such important classes of words as those concerned with numbers, metals, and colours.

The Turkic dialects, on the other hand, present a recognisable connection with the Mongol language proper, spoken from Manchuria to the borders of Russia. The oldest dialect is said to be the Buriat, of which a grammar and vocabulary were composed by Castren. In grammatical structure these two groups of language are closely connected. The relationship of the Dravidian and Kolarian languages of India to the Turkic and Akkadian is also traceable in grammar and in vocabulary; while the Burmese and Siamese are in like manner comparable with the non-Aryan languages of India; and, as recently shown (by Mr Sterndale in 1891), the Polynesian and Australian languages compare with the Siamese.

Chinese is often called a "monosyllabic language," but the term is misleading, as it only applies—as in other languages—to the roots. The population of China contains many distinct elements; and under the name of Chinese many distinct dialects are commonly grouped together. The civilising element appears to have come mainly from Turkestan (the Khitai) and Mongolia; while a large element of population also entered China from Thibet, Burmah, and Siam, at an early historic period. The modern Mandarin language, when compared with the Cantonese, which is said to be the most ancient dialect, is at once seen to have suffered so much from phonetic decay as to be unreliable for purposes of comparison; and our earliest information as to Chinese speech is so late as to render the study of the affiliation of this language peculiarly difficult. Comparisons between Chinese and Akkadian have been made by Lenormant and later scholars, which in some cases are striking, but often illusory. The ultimate connection of Mongol and Chinese speech is, however, traceable through the Manchu, which, as Lenormant shows (Magic, English edition), presents many peculiarities of grammar found in Akkadian.

The American languages (see Greg's 'Comparative Philology,' 1893) present various phases of agglutination, the Otomi approaching the Chinese, while others are more elaborate.

A large vocabulary, relating to very common objects and actions, connects together the languages of North, Central, and Southern America, and also connects them with Mongolic speech. America appears to have been first peopled by uncivilised tribes who used Mongolic words for "dog," "boat," "sea," and "snow," and came apparently from the north. They were followed within historic times by other races—such as the Toltecs, Azteks, and Peruvians—whose languages and civilisation alike connect them more closely with the extreme east of Asia than with any other part of the world.

The Semitic languages form a small and closely connected group, which is more advanced in grammatical structure than any other. The roots are, as a rule, bisyllabic; but it has long been recognised that these answer to the secondary roots found in Aryan languages, and that they are indeed often the same, while the original roots, as in other cases, were monosyllabic; and these may be traced in the imperative of verbs formed from weak or reduplicated roots.

The comparison of Egyptian with Semitic speech extends to grammatical structure, pronouns, and other important classes of words—such as those for colour—although the ancient Egyptian language is grammatically less advanced than even the oldest Semitic dialects. The old language received large additions by direct borrowing from Aramaic and from Mongol speech in the Hyksos period; but the vocabulary includes also a large proportion of words for common objects and actions which cannot be supposed to have been so borrowed, and which show a clear connection with Asiatic vocabularies of the earliest age. The Coptic is the direct descendant of the Egyptian; but Champollion observed that other Berber languages of North Africa showed connection with Egyptian, and a study of Berber grammars and vocabularies shows that this is the case, and also connects with these the ancient Guancho language of the Canary Islands. Even the Hottentot and Bushman languages were thought by the late Mr Bertin to indicate a connection with Egypt.

The study of African languages is rendered extremely difficult by their rapid change from generation to generation;

but the opinion of scholars appears to favour an ultimate, though remote, connection with Semitic speech through the Egyptian. Nearly half the great continent is covered by races speaking languages of the Bantu group, and tracing their origin to the north-east — Abyssinia and the Soudan. The Amharic language results from the admixture with African speech of the Sabean or Southern Arabic, and the Sabean in Abyssinia is traceable as a pure language of the conquering Arabs in Africa from the second century B.C. down to the fifth century A.D.

The comparison of about 170 ancient monosyllabic roots, common to Aryan and Semitic speech, and found also in Egyptian and Akkadian, will be found in the paper quoted at the beginning of this note. These roots, with many nouns relating to common objects, also recur in the American vocabularies in all parts of that continent; and although the subject is still in its infancy, the reduction of all human speech to a common origin, and to simple monosyllabic roots of mimetic value, seems already to be clearly indicated, by comparison of the results reached separately by scholars working on each class of languages, and independently of each other.

The Babylonian Flood Story.—The most recent translation by Mr T. G. Pinches of this famous tablet, first rendered by Fox Talbot and G. Smith, will be found in Dr H. H. Wright's 'Bible Reader's Manual,' p. 139, second edition. The flood, which frightened the gods themselves, is said to have increased for seven days (cf. Gen. viii. 1, 2). The Babylonian Noah (whose name is doubtful) built a ship (*elippu*) and placed in it "the seeds of life." It was caulked with bitumen (see Gen. vi. 15), and contained the family of the hero, his slaves, his silver and gold, with cattle and other beasts. The ship landed on the mountain of Nizir (see Gen. viii. 4). On the seventh day a dove was sent out, and finding no resting-place, returned (see Gen. viii. 8). A swallow was sent out next, and returned; and after that a raven, which did not return (see Gen. viii. 7). The hero then issued from the ship and offered sacrifice (Gen. viii. 21).

This account of the Deluge, though at present only known in Semitic speech, is believed to be of Akkadian origin. It is only quite recently that the Creation tablet has been found in a bilingual text—Akkadian and Assyrian—by Mr T. G. Pinches, and this discovery renders it probable that the Babylonian flood story is also a translation. It forms the eleventh tablet of a series of twelve, giving the adventures of a hero whose name is very variously transcribed. The other stories are mythical, including the strange figure of Ea-bani, a minotaur friendly to the hero, with legends which recall Greek myths such as that of Actæon.

The Mexican deluge story, in which Cox-Cox escaped to the mountain Colhuacan, probably reached America from Eastern Asia. In language, calendar, rites, symbolism, and customs, the civilised races of America—known to the Chinese Buddhists of the fifth century A.D.—are more closely connected with the extreme east of Asia than with any other civilisation. The Indian deluge is noticed in a Purana of uncertain date. The Chinese legend refers to a great river-flood; the Persian to a severe winter, whence Yima escaped in his *vara* or enclosure (Vendidad I.)—probably traceable to the age of Cyrus. The Celtic story is not traceable to any great age. The Greek deluge of Deucalion was derived apparently from the Phœnicians.

CHAPTER II.

THE PATRIARCHS.

When history first opens to us on the monuments three great races are found, in Western Asia and in Egypt, to have already attained to civilised life, while farther from the centre the Aryan and the Negro remained barbarians. The Egyptian race appears to have been the first to migrate from the common home, and its civilisation in the age of the pyramid-builders was already complete. The age to which the early wooden and alabaster statues carry us back can only be roughly estimated at not more than 3000 B.C. The true Egyptian language, though far less developed than that of the Semitic races, still bears so close a relation to theirs, in grammar and in vocabulary, as to render an original connection certain. The hieroglyphic system also shows an original connection (especially in numerals and in certain signs for country, deity, &c.) with the Asiatic systems. But many centuries of separation must have elapsed, before the time of the earliest known records, to account for the wide differences in language and writing between the Egyptians and their kinsmen in Asia.

The Mongol race, represented by the Akkadians who had spread all over Mesopotamia, was the first ruling and civilised people in Asia. The monuments of Gudea at the city of Zirghul, between the Tigris and the Euphrates, show us that about 2700 B.C. the Akkadian princes already ruled over a wide region in Western Asia. They had conquered Elam—or Western Persia —and were in trading relations with regions near the Caucasus, with Phœnicia, and with Sinai. They brought gold-dust from Upper Egypt, and sailed round the whole of Arabia. They had a calendar of twelve lunar months, and a complete system of writing. They knew all the metals, and carved in granite and in alabaster. They built great pyramids of brick in bitumen cement, and palaces adorned with granite statues. They tilled the land with hoes and ploughs, and built ships with sails. It is doubtful whether already the Akkadian civilisation is not to be traced even earlier than that of Egypt, with which it had much in common.

The language of the Akkadians was a primitive Mongol tongue, of which the nearest living representative is the pure Turkic speech of Central Asia.[1] The Mongolian proper, the Chinese, Burmese, and early Indian languages are more remotely comparable with it in vocabulary and in grammar. The racial type of the Akkadians was also Mongol, and by race and language they were akin to the Hittites and other tribes in Palestine and Asia Minor. The religion of all these tribes was the same, and re-

[1] See note, p. 31.

sembled that of later Mongols. Heaven, earth, ocean, and hell were peopled by them with countless spirits good and bad, over whom presided the two great gods—the "spirit of heaven" and the "spirit of earth."

It was from the Akkadians that the first Semitic peoples borrowed their earliest civilisation and earliest written character. It is not until the time of Hammurapaltu, the Cassite (or Cushite) conqueror of Babylon and of Syria, that the Semitic language of Chaldea

Hittites from Abu Simbel.

begins to be used in historic records side by side with the earlier Akkadian. The home of the Semitic race was, however, near to that of the ruling Akkadians. The evidence of common words, found in all Semitic languages, shows that the forefathers of the race came from a region where barley and wheat were grown, where the stork existed beside great rivers, and where the olive, fig, pomegranate, and vine flourished. They knew the horse, the ass, the goat, sheep, and dog. They had domestic cattle, and also knew the wild bull and the lion. The pelican is yet more distinctive of their home; but the panther, fox, hyena, bear, wild-cat, boar, stag, and gazelle, with the wild ass of the Aramean plains, were also early named. It is impossible to find any region which would fit all these requirements in Arabia, which some scholars have regarded as the Semitic cradle. The plains of Assyria and the foothills of the Taurus, the valleys of the Euphrates and Tigris, and the Armenian mountains, seem to be clearly indicated as the first home of the race which afterwards spread to Syria, and yet later to Arabia. About 2000 B.C. they carried with them to the West their syllabic system of writing—originally borrowed from the Akkadians—and a singularly perfect Aramean language, which appears with a completely developed grammar in the texts of Hammurapaltu about 2100 B.C.

The original Egyptians were followed to the Delta about the same time by mingled tribes, Mongol and Semitic. The ruling race, usually known as Hyksos, called themselves the Men or Minyans,[1] and their broad-cheeked racial type connects them with the Akkadians and with the later Minni or Minyans in Armenia, who spoke in the fifteenth century B.C. a language akin to that of the Akkadians and Hittites. The condition of Western Asia about 2100 B.C. appears to have resulted from the migration of Semitic tribes into Syria, over whom, as well as over the mixed Mongol and Semitic races in Mesopotamia, Hammurapaltu at Babylon claimed to rule—a rule

[1] See note, p. 31.

no doubt only maintained, as in later times, by constant and distant expeditions. On the east Eriaku, his contemporary in Larsa, had been conquered by this great monarch; and the two empires of the earliest historic age are those of Babylon—under the Cushites, and of Egypt—under the kindred Minyans. The Semitic peoples appear to have been only divided tribes, under local leaders, owning allegiance to Babylon; while the farthest Egyptian outpost seems to have been at the turquoise mines in Sinai.

Such is the general result obtained from study of the Zirghul texts, the early inscriptions of Egypt, and the records of Hammurapaltu. It casts an unexpected light on the Hebrew records from the days of Nimrod to those of Abraham, and it serves to fix independently the age of the Hebrew patriarch contemporary with Hammurapaltu and Eriaku—Amraphel and Arioch of the Hebrew. The building of a great tower in Mesopotamia with brick and bitumen is recorded in Genesis as occurring at Babylon; and at Zirghul the remains of such a tower, with texts which show that it was built several centuries before the date given to Abraham, have actually been found. These towers, or *ziggurs* as the Akkadians called them, were stepped pyramids with a shrine on the top. They resembled the Egyptian pyramids except in orientation, and served as altars to the "spirit of heaven." They must have been familiar to the Hebrew ancestors long before they left their home in Chaldea; but they continued in existence to a much later age, and were once again seen by the children of the Captivity in Babylon.

The list of races in Genesis presents us, however, with conditions which ceased to exist in later times. Asiatic man is there divided into three great groups, which clearly answer to the three races of science—Aryan, Mongol, and Semitic. The history of the early Aryans is unrecorded, for the art of writing only reached them later from Syria; but the evidence of language shows how early the Slav and Celtic stocks spread to Greece, to Asia Minor, and to Italy, from Southern Russia. Egyptian monuments of the fourteenth and thirteenth century B.C. present us with the Danai or Greeks and other light-haired, blue-eyed peoples, who were then invading Syria and pushing south to the confines of Egypt.[1] Under this head (Japhet, the "fair" race) the Hebrew writer classes Cimmerians and Medes, Ionians, and the Tuplai and Moschi of Armenia. The Medes were already met in this region by the Assyrians in the ninth century B.C., and are well known to have been an Aryan people, who may have dwelt for centuries in Georgia before the Assyrians pushed north to the mountains round Lake Van. The other Aryan tribes of Genesis include Ashkenaz and Togarmah in Armenia, Elishah (the Alasiya of the monuments) in Cilicia, with Tarshish, Cyprus, and Rhodes. At the time when the tenth chapter of Genesis was written the Aryans had spread all over Asia Minor and as far south as Cyprus.

The second race of Genesis is Ham (the "dark" people), who ruled in Cush and in Egypt, and to whom the earliest Canaanites were kin, as well as the people of Akkad in

[1] See note, p. 32.

Mesopotamia and Elamite tribes on the Persian Gulf. The Akkadian kingdom is said to have spread northwards from Babylon to Assyria, where Nineveh was built later than Babylon. At present our monumental notices carry back the history of Babylon to 2300 B.C., and that of Nineveh to about 1600 B.C.; but even this later date is earlier than that at which Genesis is supposed to have been written by those who place its antiquity at the highest. The southern branch of Ham includes the Egyptians and Philistines, with other unknown tribes. The early Canaanites are said to have spread from the north to Gaza, and first among them the Hittites are reckoned. Such connection between the races of Chaldea (the Cushites) and those of Egypt (the Minyans) ceased to be truly racial about 1700 B.C., when the first great Nubian dynasty expelled the Asiatics. The writer in Genesis refers to an early age when as yet the Hebrew tribes had not entered Canaan; but he groups with other Canaanites the Amorites, who—as known to us in the fifteenth century B.C.—were not a Mongol but an Aramean people, speaking the same language used by Babylonians and Assyrians, and using the same character in writing. Already, therefore—as in the Hyksos period in Egypt—the population of Canaan appears, according to the statement of Genesis, to have included mingled tribes of the families of Shem and Ham.

The third race of Genesis is that of Shem (the "brown"), and includes nations in Elam, Assyria, Lydia, and Aram, with tribes in Arabia as far south as Sheba and Yemen. The colonisation of Arabia seems to have been pushed along both shores of the great peninsula: for in the earliest known texts of this region the dialects of the west are nearest to west Semitic speech, and those of the far east (in Hazarmaveth or Hadramaut) nearest to the eastern Aramaic; while the short texts of Northern Arabia — of which the earliest belongs to about the fourth century B.C.—present us with an Aramaic dialect similar to that of Syria and of Petra. The limit of geographical knowledge in Genesis is marked by Persia on the east and Ionia on the west, by Armenia on the north and by Egypt on the south. The evidence of inscriptions shows us that Armenia, Assyria, and Babylon were already in constant communication with Egypt in the fifteenth century B.C., and that both Elam (or Persia) and Egypt were known to the Akkadians, with Sinai and Syria, even ten centuries earlier. It also shows us the establishment of Aryan tribes in Asia Minor at least as early as 1400 B.C.

The geography and races of Genesis alike, therefore, belong to the earliest historic age. If, as some scholars have supposed, this famous chapter was penned in later years of Persian rule, it is difficult to suppose that, under such changed conditions, the history of the diffusion of earlier races would have still been known, and the writer succeed in escaping from anachronisms which would at once betray his age. The rude Aryan tribes of Armenia had then been conquered. The Persians—who find no place in this scheme of races—were dominant in Babylon, and far westwards in Ionia and Cyprus. The old Mongol rulers of Egypt had long been forgotten; the princes of Philistia bore Semitic names; the Hittites had been exterminated by Assyria; and the names of Canaanite tribes, as existing in Palestine, are unnoticed by Nehemiah or by Ezra. Colonists from Hamath and from yet farther east had long been planted in Samaria, and Arab tribes had invaded the north and had settled round Petra. The old world known to the writer in Genesis had long since passed away when the Jews returned from captivity, but in the days of Moses the conditions of race and language differed little from those set forth in the table of races in Genesis.

The cities mentioned in this chapter are also very ancient. Babylon and Nineveh were built long before the Exodus, and Arvad, Zemar, Hamath, Arkah, Sidon, Gerar, and Gaza are mentioned on monuments of the sixteenth and fifteenth centuries B.C. Damascus, noticed in a later chapter, is equally ancient, being mentioned in 1600 B.C.; Jebus or Jerusalem (by its latter name) in the fifteenth century B.C.; and Dothan a century earlier.[1] Haran also in northern Mesopotamia is once mentioned in the fifteenth century B.C.; and only one town—Dan at the sources of the Jordan—bears a name which, according to the Bible itself, was given it in the times of the Judges. There is no allusion in Genesis to later cities, such as Tirzah or Samaria; and it is remarkable that among Phœnician towns Sidon stands alone, and its

[1] See note, p. 32.

later rival Tyre is unnoticed. Tyre, however, is traced on monuments to the fifteenth century B.C., and is perhaps omitted, with Gebal, Batrun, and other early Syrian cities, as having been founded by Semitic, not by Hamitic, emigrants. Excepting Dan, the only indication of a late date in Genesis is the notice of Rameses in the time of Jacob; for if scholars be right in supposing that this name cannot be older than the time of the nineteenth dynasty in Egypt, the narrative would thereby be dated as having been completed not earlier than about 1300 B.C. Such a date would suit not only the notice of the Aryans in Asia Minor, but also that of Dan under its later name.

The Hebrew ancestor is represented to us as leaving Ur, the great city near the mouth of the Euphrates, and travelling north to Haran, near the foot of the Taurus, whence he crossed the river and came south to Central Palestine, and to the desert of Beersheba, visiting Egypt, then ruled by Asiatics. Phœnician tradition of a later age traced the origin of this kindred Semitic race of the Syrian shores to the same region near the Persian Gulf; and it is clear that any tribe which meant to enter Canaan from Chaldea must have crossed the Euphrates far to the north. The Syrian desert is an impassable barrier, which only disappears north of Hamath, and where Carchemish guarded the fords of the Euphrates. All the great expeditions of the eighteenth dynasty from Egypt followed the same highway to Carchemish, when attempting to subdue Assyria, that Abraham is said to have followed from Haran towards the Delta. The fact that the earliest Semitic tribes—Amorites and others—came from Assyria is now attested by the evidence of language and of writing; and to suppose that the first emigrants in Palestine were Arabs from the south is to set up a theory based on no foundation, and contradicting the evidence that we possess.

The date of the first Hebrew migration is fixed by the names of Amraphel and Arioch,[1] kings of Shinar (Mesopotamia), and of Ellasar, which was apparently Larsa. These monarchs—the Hammurapaltu and Eriaku of the monuments—were contemporaries who, according to the monumental canon of Babylonian kings, lived about 2100 B.C. The former speaks of himself, in one of his texts, as ruling in the Phœnician regions; and the incursions of the Akkadians into Sinai are mentioned some centuries earlier. The account in Genesis of Amraphel's great raid on Bashan, Moab, and the regions round Petra, and of his retreat towards Damascus, thus fully accords with the scanty notices on monuments as yet discovered. Even the lands of Ham and Hobah, which are noticed in the same narrative, have been discovered on monuments as places near Damascus attacked by the Hittites in the fifteenth century B.C.

Not less interesting is the allusion to Hittite tribes as living in Hebron in the time of Abraham, and to their settled life in cities, and their wealth. The Hittites were driven out of Southern Palestine about 1600 B.C. by Thothmes III. In the Book of Joshua they appear as

[1] See note, p. 33.

inhabitants of Northern Syria, and this was their home from about 1500 to 700 B.C. But in the lowest strata of the ruins of Lachish, not far west of Hebron, a Hittite seal has been found, with others bearing titles of the Egyptian eighteenth dynasty, and the seal of Teie, consort of Amenophis III. The mention of Hittites in the far south thus points to an early age, and agrees with the contemporary notice of Amraphel and Abraham.

There are several other indications in the history of the Patriarchs on which the monuments throw light. The jewels offered to Rebecca recall those, of which a long list exists, which were brought from Armenia by Tadukhepa, the Mongol bride of Amenophis IV. The Midianite caravan which brought Joseph to Egypt reminds us of the many recorded expeditions of ambassadors bearing presents to Egypt in the fifteenth century B.C.; but the merchandise that the Midianites bore—styrax, balm, and cistus gum—like the pistachio nuts of Jacob's present, are natural products of Palestine itself. The difference noted between the Hebrew speech of Jacob and the Aramean of Laban is illustrated by the Aramean language of existing Amorite letters, as contrasted with the language of the Bible.

Viewed in the light of extant monuments, the story of Genesis presents to us a true picture of the state of Asia before the great Egyptian conquests of the sixteenth century of our era.

NOTES TO CHAPTER II.

The Akkadian Language.—The original discovery of a non-Semitic language in Mesopotamia was made by Sir H. Rawlinson. The subject is exhaustively treated by F. Lenormant ('Études Accadiennes'), by aid of about thirty bilingual texts in Assyrian and Akkadian; and the Mongolic character of this ancient tongue is established by the peculiarities of its grammatical structure. The present writer ('Journal of the Royal Asiatic Society,' October 1893) has endeavoured to show that out of the small Akkadian vocabulary as yet known some 200 words are closely comparable with pure Turkish,—including numerals and names of colours,—and that the Akkadian noun possessed also the eight cases of the Turkish. Further materials have been found at Tell Loh (the ancient Zirghul) in the shape of semi-historic, semi-religious texts on statues of Gudea, dating probably from 2700 B.C. (De Sarzek, 'Découvertes en Chaldée'), and in the new bilingual Creation tablet (T. G. Pinches, 'Journal of the Royal Asiatic Society,' July 1891).

The Hyksos.—The *Men* or Hyksos are said to have come from a country near Assyria, and east of Ruten or Syria, and ruled in the Delta for 511 years as the fifteenth and sixteenth dynasties, according to Manetho. George the Syncellus (sixth century A.D.) believed that Joseph came to Egypt in the reign of Apophis or Apepi. This king worshipped Set, who was a Hittite god, according to the records of Rameses II. (see Brugsch, 'Hist. Egypt,' vol. i. p. 239). The term *Men*, and the geographical indication, connect the Hyksos with the Minyans of classical writers who lived near Lake Van. About 1500 B.C. Dusratta, the ruler of Mitani (or Matiene) in Armenia, wrote to Egypt a letter in his own language, from which it appears that his race was also Minyan (see the paper by the present author in the 'Journal of the Royal Asiatic Society,' October 1893). The language of this letter is clearly

Mongolic, and connected with the Akkadian, and with the Hittite, as shown by another letter in the same collection (No. 10, Berlin), which was written by Tarkondara, the Hittite prince of Rezeph. These indications, taken in connection with the portrait statues of the Hyksos kings in the Gizeh Museum, point to a Mongolic race from Armenia ruling for five centuries in Egypt, and akin to the Mongols of Syria and Chaldea.

The Aryan Invaders of Egypt.—The casts and descriptions by Dr Flinders Petrie show that these invaders were a light-coloured people with fair hair and blue eyes. There has been much controversy as to the identification of many of the tribes named in the texts. The great league against Rameses II. about 1328 B.C. (see Brugsch, 'Hist. Egypt,' vol. ii. p. 44) included, in addition to the Hittites and men of Aradus, Aleppo, and Aram-Naharaim, others named *Leka* (Ligyes), *Dardani* (Dardanians), &c., "from the extreme end of the sea." The league against Mineptah in 1300 B.C. ('Hist. Egypt,' vol. ii. p. 116), included the *Leku* (who are also noticed in Asia Minor in the Tell Amarna letters), with the *Shairdana* (possibly Sardians) and other "people of the north." The league against Rameses III., in 1200 B.C., included the *Danau*, Danai or Greeks, with others who came both by sea and by land (p. 147). The names and the types of these invaders are alike Aryan. The *Pulesta*, or *Purosata*, who accompanied the last invaders, are variously thought to have been Philistines, and inhabitants of Prusia or Broussa.

Cities taken by Thothmes III. in Palestine.—This famous list of 119 towns in Palestine, conquered about 1600 B.C. by Thothmes III., includes many which are mentioned in the Old Testament. It was studied by Mariette at Karnak. The latest identifications will be found in the volume of translations of the Tell Amarna tablets, published by the present author in 1893. Among the more certainly identified Bible cities are Megiddo, Dothan, Rabbith, Damascus, Edrei,

Abila, Hammath, Madon, Lasharon, Ashtaroth, Hazor, Adami, Shunem, Achshaph, Taanach, Kadesh, Anaharath, and Nekeb, in Bashan and Galilee; Joppa, Lydda, Ono, Shochoh, Naamah, Saphir, Rakkon, Gerar, Aroer, Rehoboth, Adoraim, Gezer, Zoreah, Engannim, and Zephathah, in the Philistine plains. The forms of the names are Aramaic rather than Hebrew, and the list gives conclusive evidence that the nomenclature is older than the Hebrew conquest, and Canaanite, not Hebrew, in origin. As regards cities farther north, Kadesh, Semyra, and Arvad are noticed in the thirtieth year of the same conqueror ('Hist. Egypt,' vol. i. p. 331), and Shinar in the thirty-third year (p. 333). Assyria gave tribute in the thirty-second year (p. 328); and Arkah, with Kadesh on the Orontes, and Tunep (Tennib), are noticed in another campaign (p. 343). Aleppo and Carchemish are also mentioned (p. 353) in the same reign. Sidon, Tyre, Accho, Semyra, Arvad, Gebal, Arkah, Beirût, and Tunep, are noticed in Phœnicia in the Tell Amarna letters, as is Damascus with the lands of Ham and Hobah; while in Philistia letters were sent from Gezer, Lachish, Joppa, Ascalon, Zoreah, and Makkedah; and Gaza is also noticed; while the letters from Jerusalem are still more important (1480-1440 B.C.).

Amraphel.—The name of this early Babylonian conqueror has been variously read Hammurabi (G. Smith), Hammuragas (Sayce), and Hammurapaltu (Hommel); while that of Eriaku has also been rendered as though a Semitic name, Aradsinu, &c. These variations are common in cases where the names are not checked by variant signs, but there is no doubt that Dr Hommel's rendering is possible, and, as compared with the Hebrew, probable. Hammurapaltu seems to have been the first great king of Babylon, and claimed to rule the land of the *Amurri* or Amorites of the Lebanon. He also made a canal in Babylonia. His principal inscription in the Semitic language is now in the Louvre. A contract tablet in the British Museum relates to the sale of a field and house in the "month Adar" during his reign, and another to "ten manehs of silver" in the reign of Eriaku. The main inscription in six columns, on a monument of black basalt, contains 126 lines of writing (see British Museum Catalogue, Nimrud gallery, pp. 16 and 75). The date of his reign is fixed by the canon of Babylonian kings, translated by Mr T. G. Pinches of the British Museum.

CHAPTER III.

THE EXODUS.

In order to compare the narrative of the Exodus with what is now known of the early history of Egypt and Syria, from monumental records, it is first necessary to know the probable date of that event. There is no notice of the Hebrews in any Egyptian record, but the relations between the native dynasties and the foreign Hyksos, and the history of the expulsion of the Asiatics by the first Nubian kings, are clearly indicated in several texts. Some writers have doubted whether Israel ever dwelt in Egypt at all, but there is no dispute as to the rule of Asiatics in the Delta from about 2200 to 1700 B.C.

The date which is commonly assumed by some Egyptian scholars is more than a century later than that given in the Bible, and Rameses II. is by them supposed to have been the great oppressor of Israel. This view was first advocated by Bunsen, but it does not rest on any statements found in Egyptian records. It was based partly on the history of Manetho—who lived in the third century B.C.—and partly on the occurrence of the name Raamses (Exod. i. 11) as that of a store-city built by

Israelites for the Pharaohs. The objections to such a view are, that it ignores the whole chronology of the Old Testament, and that the period is not one suitable to the event. The Hebrews appear in Palestine much earlier, according to the tablets of the king of Jerusalem who wrote to Amenophis early in the fifteenth century. The notice of Raamses has no force, since the land of Rameses is noticed in Genesis (xlvii. 11) in the time of Jacob. The monuments tell us nothing of the Exodus, but such evidence as they afford favours a date more in accord with the statements of the Bible.

The author of the Book of Kings states that 480 years (according to the Hebrew text) elapsed between the fourth year of Solomon and the conquest of Palestine by Joshua (1 Kings vi. 1); and Solomon reigned forty years and was succeeded by Rehoboam (1 Kings xi. 42), who was attacked by Shishak king of Egypt (1 Kings xiv. 25), whose reign is independently fixed. Exact chronology at this early period is not yet attainable, but the accession of Solomon must roughly have coincided with the year 1000 B.C., which would carry back the Exodus to about 1520 B.C. This lapse of time is independently checked by the statement that Israel had been settled for three centuries in Gilead in Jephthah's time (Judges xi. 26), and by the statement in the New Testament (Acts xiii. 19-21) that Israel was ruled by Judges for 450 years. The date of Solomon is further checked by the details of chronology between his time and that of Sargon's conquest of Samaria, and of Sennacherib's attack on

Jerusalem, which latter event took place about 260 years after Solomon's death, and coincided with the year 702 B.C. When we consider the details contained in the Books of Samuel and Judges, we find that a complete through reckoning is not possible, since the length of Saul's reign is unknown. The rule of Eli, Samuel, and David covered a century. The details of the rule of the Judges amount to 370 years, and Jephthah's rule begins about 320 years after the conquest. The total leaves us ten years, to include Saul's reign, and is as close as could be expected to the through reckonings in each case. It seems clear that Hebrew historians all believed that nearly five centuries elapsed between the conquest and the death of David; and we have no reason to doubt that the Bible record is to be preferred to the much later and less reliable statements of Manetho. It is impossible to crowd the details of the Bible chronology into the three centuries between Rameses II. and Shishak, and Bunsen's hasty theory must therefore be abandoned, in view of increased monumental information.

The early date thus fixed for the Exodus — about 1520 B.C. — also agrees with that to be assigned to Abraham as a contemporary with Amraphel, whose reign commenced in 2120 B.C. Out of the six centuries intervening 430 years were passed by Israel in Egypt, which leaves the very natural interval of 170 years for the lives of three generations—Abraham, Isaac, and Jacob—in Palestine. The date of the going down of Israel into Egypt is thus carried back to about 1950 B.C. The Book of Exodus states that another king arose "who knew not Joseph," and we may understand that under a new dynasty the favour formerly shown to the Hebrews was changed to a bondage which led finally to their leaving Egypt.

The relations of the Egyptians to the Asiatics of the Delta, and to the Canaanites in Palestine and in Syria, can be independently studied on the monuments. About 1600 B.C. Egyptian dates begin to be fixed with some accuracy by astronomical statements which can be calculated from fixed data.[1] Hence the results given by Dr Brugsch rest on a firm basis, and may be used for comparison with Bible dates. The monumental notices of the Hyksos show them to have been in constant relations with Asia: "all good things came from the north" in the reign of Apepi, and the invading Minyans adored no Egyptian gods, but worshipped Set, who is monumentally known to have been also a Hittite deity. The descent of Hebrews into Egypt, in the time of this friendly dynasty, presents no natural objection, nor is the rise of a Hebrew vizir to power unnatural when Egypt was ruled by Asiatics. But about 1700 B.C. the new Nubian dynasty attained power and waged war against the Hyksos. Under the famous queen Hatasu the power of the native race increased steadily, and Egyptian fleets sailed down the Red Sea to Somali-land, while the riches of the Soudan were brought by the Nile boats to Thebes. The reign of Thothmes III. began

[1] See note, p. 51.

about 1600 B.C., when the Asiatics were driven out and the conquest of the Syrian shores effected after a terrible battle against Hittites and Phœnicians at Megiddo in Central Palestine. The famous list of 119 towns conquered in Palestine by Thothmes III. includes all those in the Philistine plains, in Lower Galilee and Sharon, and in Bashan, as far as Damascus. The conquest was pushed north along the shores of Phœnicia to the inland plain of Kadesh on the Orontes, to Carchemish on the Euphrates, and to the plains of Assyria south of the Taurus. The Egyptians held all the trade-route between Haran and Gaza, with that running from Carmel by Megiddo to Ashtaroth-Carnaim and Damascus. They had posts, garrisoned by chariots, in all the plains, and exacted regular rations from the Canaanites for their troops at every "resting-place" along the roads. Only the mountains of Hebron and Shechem escaped the power of their chariot forces, with the rugged regions of Edom, Moab, and Gilead. The old posts in Sinai were garrisoned with archers, and Egypt became the leading power in Western Asia.

The conquests thus gained were retained during the long and peaceful reign of Amenophis III. The Pharaohs were allied by marriage to the kings of Armenia and of Babylon, and constant embassies went to and fro between these countries and Egypt. The "kings of Canaan" were recognised as "slaves" of Egypt; and Dusratta, from Armenia, conquered the rebel Hittites, receiving part of the north of Syria as the dowry of Tadukhepa, his daughter—the bride of Amenophis IV., then heir to the throne of Thebes. His sister Gilukhepa was married to Amenophis III. himself; and Teie, the chief wife and mother of the heir, seems also to have been his relative, if we may judge from the familiar letters which passed between the two when Amenophis III. "went to his fate," and was mourned by Dusratta as an old and faithful friend.

But in the last years of Amenophis III., and during the reign of his son and heir, a long-threatened rebellion broke out in Syria about 1480 B.C. The Hittites conquered all the plains south of Kadesh, as far as Damascus and Ashtaroth-Carnaim in Bashan, and remained independent for more than a century. The Amorites of Tennib in the Lebanon captured Semyra on the coast of Phœnicia, and swept down on the cities of Batrun, Gebal, Beirut, Sidon, and Tyre. The Egyptian forces were driven out, and Tyre was besieged by Aziru the Amorite, aided by the fleet of Arvad. In the same years (during the lifetime at least of the same Egyptian general Yankhamu) troubles in Southern Palestine also arose. The Philistine chiefs of Gezer, Ascalon, Lachish, and other cities had for several generations owned the Pharaohs as their overlords, and forces of chariots garrisoned their towns. Even in Jerusalem itself Egyptian bowmen supported the Amorite ruler, and all the borders of the Hebron hills were guarded by Egyptian posts. But a fierce people from the East, coming from Seir, fighting at Ajalon, reducing to tribute Gezer, Ascalon, Lachish, Keilah, and other towns, overturned the power of Egypt in Jerusalem and in the Philistine plains. These facts we learn from the extant letters of the princes of Philistia and Jerusalem; and the name of the conquerors is often given as the *Abiri* or Hebrews. The power of Egypt rapidly declined. Amenophis IV. is believed to have been murdered, and his successor Horus is addressed by an Assyrian prince, who speaks of the interruption of relations between his country and Egypt. The great eighteenth dynasty came to an end, and when, under Seti I., a more vigorous rule was established, the conquest of the trade-route, and the subjugation of the Hittites, had to be once more undertaken from the far south—the first battles being at Sharuhen and Ascalon. In spite, however, of the success of Rameses II., about 1350 B.C., the power of Egypt was never fully re-established. In the reign of Mineptah the Asiatics again pressed down on the Delta. The Shasu or shepherds of Sinai were "allowed to pass from Edom," and to pasture their flocks in the Delta; and fierce invaders from Asia Minor (Greeks and other Aryans) attacked the Hittites, and fought their way along the shores of Palestine to the mouths of the Nile.

This brief review of the actual condition of Palestine between 1600 and 1300 B.C., which is established by the Egyptian texts, and by the Tell Amarna letters on tablets of brick, found in the library of the Theban kings, shows us very clearly that the reign of Mineptah was not a period when an exodus of Asiatics took place, but, on the contrary, one when they were once more invading the

Delta in a time when Egyptian rule was weak. It shows us that from the time of Ahmes (1700 B.C.) down to that of Amenophis IV., the power of Egypt was paramount in Palestine, attaining its height between 1600 and 1500 B.C. After this date it was destroyed by native rebellions, and only for a time re-established—a century and a half later—by Rameses II., after whom it passed away for ever. It is just during this time of rebellion that the name of the Hebrews first meets us on the monuments about 1480 B.C., and the date coincides with that which is to be derived from the Bible for the Hebrew conquest, 480 years before the reign of Solomon.

The descent of Israel into Egypt thus coincided with the rule of the Hyksos or Minyan dynasty; and for 250 years they would have flourished under friendly Asiatic rulers. But the "new king" (Exod. i. 8) who arose was Ahmes from Thebes, and the oppression and expulsion of the Asiatics was the task of the first rulers of the eighteenth or Nubian dynasty, whose capitals were at Tell Amarna—half-way between Thebes and Memphis—and at Thebes itself. The sculptures of Thothmes III. were set up at Thebes, and the more northern palace seems to have been built by Amenophis III., and remained the royal residence till the reign of Horus. The Egyptian outposts, it is well to note, were held at the copper mines of Sinai till the time of Thothmes IV., but abandoned during the great rebellion. The Exodus (if occurring about 1520 B.C.) coincides with the reign of this monarch, who pursued his father's policy in Asia; and the greatest oppressor of the Hebrews was the greatest of Egyptian conquerors—Thothmes III.

But it is evident that if this date be established, the immediate conquest of Palestine by the Hebrews was impossible for at least forty years. Gaza, Ascalon, and other cities on the "way of the Philistines" were strongly held during most of the reign of Amenophis III. by forces of chariots. It was only in the desert of Sinai, or among the kindred tribes of Edom, that the fugitives could find refuge, until the great opportunity came in 1480 B.C., when all Palestine rose in rebellion against the weak son of Amenophis III. If it be admitted that Israel descended into Egypt in the time of the Hyksos, it follows that their expulsion would most naturally be ordered by the Nubian kings who drove the Asiatics from the Delta. It also follows that the Hebrew conquest could not have happened before the power of Egypt was broken half a century later.

The geography of the Exodus route is the next question of importance in judging of the narrative. A list of stations in the desert is said in the Bible to have been written down by Moses himself (Num. xxxiii.), and the possibility of tracing on the ground the line of Hebrew migration will much affect our reading of the whole account. As regards the numbers of the Hebrews great difficulties arise, which were studied by Bishop Colenso with much minuteness. As they now stand it is difficult to regard them as historical; but numbers are more subject to alteration than any other statements.[1] The various versions of the Bible show that much alteration was made by scribes, and usually the later numbers are increased by hundreds, or even thousands, as compared with the Hebrew text. The question of numbers is one, therefore, which it is probably hopeless to treat with our present sources of knowledge.

This, however, is not the case as regards geography, on which subject exploration of the ground has cast a clear and certain light. It is generally agreed that the land of Goshen was that part of the Delta which had been ruled by the Hyksos or Minyans, including Zoan (the present ruin of Sân), which was called later the city of Rameses, and Succoth (now Tell el Maskhuta) on the way leading to Gaza. The route of the Exodus led along the valley which now reaches the lakes at Ismailieh, and which may at that time have been an arm of the Nile. Here Israel "turned" to the south towards the wilderness, and crossed the shoals at the head of the Red Sea. The falling tide, in the uncertain April weather, was driven back by a "contrary wind," and the passage lay between the lagoons, so that the waters were a "defence" on either side against attack. The change of wind and rising of the tide are recorded to have delayed the Egyptian pursuit, and led to the disaster in which they perished.

The exact site of the great mountain Horeb or Sinai is not noticed, but it was "eleven days' journey" (Deut. i. 2) from Kadesh Barnea on the Edomite border. It was also

[1] See note, p. 51.

on the "west side of the desert" (Exod. iii. 1), and only about "three days'" rapid march (Exod. v. 3) from Egypt. Josephus the Jewish historian says that Sinai was the highest mountain in the desert, and all these indications point to the accepted site at Jebel Mûsa—the highest and most remarkable mountain block in the desert. The details of the Hebrew march, from their first camp east of the Red Sea, confirm this conclusion, although but few of the stations have been certainly recovered. The first camp was probably by the springs now called Ayûn Mûsa, about ten miles from the point of passage. Their journey, encumbered as they were with women, children, flocks, and herds, was slow, and a day's march cannot have exceeded ten or fifteen miles at most. A long halt was made at Elim, and Sinai was not reached till May. Here Israel abode some two months, and Kadesh Barnea on the east of the desert was not approached till early in autumn. At this city the Hebrews lingered "many days," apparently a whole year, before they began to wander in the Arabah, visiting various camps between Mount Hor and Elath on the Gulf of Akabah. Their nomad life in this region is stated to have continued more than thirty-seven years, and in April, on the thirty-ninth Passover after that first held in Egypt, they returned to Kadesh Barnea, where Aaron died in July. In spite of a victory over the Amorites at Arad—on the plateau east of Beer-sheba—the south border of Palestine was found to be too strong for their attack, and they retraced their steps to circle round the Edomites of Kadesh Barnea, entering

Moab by a painful journey over the desert plateau. Zered, east of the Dead Sea, was reached in the autumn, but the next five months witnessed a rapid raid over Moab, Gilead, and Bashan, until the fortieth Passover was held, after the death of Moses and the passage of the Jordan, at Gilgal, east of Jericho.

That Hebrew tribes should have been able to penetrate through these regions by the usual route to Edom, required the existence of springs of water such as are rarely found on the Tih plateau north of Sinai. In the Arabah itself, south of Kadesh Barnea, no such difficulty arose, since there is an abundant supply both at Petra and also near the site of Ezion Geber. This region, as well as Sinai itself, and that farther west in Wâdy Feirân which has now a fine stream, has always supported a nomadic population, owning camels, flocks, and herds. There is no physical reason why Hebrew tribes might not have lived on for any length of time at such centres, until the occasion for conquest came with the decay of the Egyptian power. The scene of their wanderings is defined (Deut. i. 1) as being in the Arabah, between Tophel (now Tufileh in Edom, south of the Arnon) and Hazeroth (Ain Hadireh), east of Sinai. The site of Kadesh Barnea, placed by Josephus near Petra, has been there shown alike by Christian and Jewish tradition, which agrees with the statement that it was on the "edge" of the Edomite dominions. Some scholars have sought to show that it was the same as the Kadesh which Hagar visited, between Beersheba and Egypt, the site of which is probably found in the present Ain Kadis in the Tih.[1] But it is certain that there were two towns of the name in this region, and the attempt to place Kadesh Barnea so far west confuses the whole of the Bible topography. Kadesh at Petra was just eleven days' ordinary journey from the traditional site of Sinai.

Leaving the first camp at Ayûn Mûsa, the Hebrews went three days' journey in the desert before they reached the bitter waters of Marah. Ain Huwârah, the usually accepted site for this camp, is thirty-seven miles (or three days' journey) from Ayûn Mûsa, and presents only a scanty supply. Elim, the next camp, where were twelve wells and seventy palms, appears to coincide with Wâdy Ghurundel, a march to the south of Ain Huwârah. It still possesses a running brook and stunted palms. The next day's journey led once more to the shores of the Red Sea, for the plain east of the Gulf of Suez here narrows —a spur of the inland hills projecting towards the shore. There is a small supply of water for sixteen miles at intervals along this route.

The exact line of march between this point and Sinai is doubtful. Four stations (Sin, Dophkah, Alush, and Rephidim) are mentioned, and the latter is usually placed at the stream of Wâdy Feirân. The total distance from the shore to Sinai is less than forty miles, giving four short marches between the four stations. At Rephidim the Amalekite attack was repulsed, and it is possible that Egyptian bowmen from the copper-mines may have

[1] See note, p. 52.

taken part in this final attempt to stop the Hebrew march.

The site of Sinai is remarkable for the broad plain to the west, stretching to the very foot of the mountain, and fitted as the camping-ground of a large force. But water is scanty, except close to the mountain, and it is possible that Israel was scattered in several small camps, assembling from some distance "at the sound of the trumpet."

Between Sinai and Moserah—at Mount Hor—sixteen stations are mentioned, which agrees with the estimated eleven days' journey of another passage. The third camp was at Hazeroth—now Ain Hadireh—which is about thirty miles from Sinai in the required direction. The sixth station from Hazeroth was Mount Shapher, which may be the present Tell el Asfar, six miles north of the Gulf of Akabah and sixty miles from Hazeroth. From Mount Shapher, so fixed, to Mount Hor is a distance of fifty-five miles, and in this section of the march seven stations are mentioned. The total distance thus agrees with the details between the known sites, giving an average daily journey of about ten miles, which in our own time is the usual limit of progress for an Arab tribe when changing camp with their families and flocks. The slow progress in the desert contrasts with the rapidity of the marches in Moab, Gilead, and Bashan; but when invading the lands of the Amorites the Hebrews left their wives and flocks in the standing camp at Shittim, under Mount Nebo.

Of the stations in the Arabah, where Israel dwelt

during the rest of the forty years, less is known. Gudgodah is probably the present Ghadaghit—a valley some twenty miles west of Mount Hor. Jotbath, a place where there were "torrents of water," appears to be the present Et Tâbah—a ruined site in the Arabah some twenty miles south of Gudgodah. The streams are here abundant, flowing towards the Gulf of Akabah. The site of Ezion Geber near Elath is fixed at 'Ain Ghudhian, north of Jotbah; and these identifications agree with the general limits of the scene of wanderings mentioned in the first verses of Deuteronomy.

The stations between Kadesh and Moab are little known; but Iim is possibly the present Aimeh—a ruin sixteen miles south of the brook Zered, which was the next camp. From Dibon in Moab to Mount Nebo the various stations coincide with well-watered valleys, and five marches covered sixty miles. There is thus throughout the itinerary nothing which causes any difficulty, either as regards distance or as regards the water-supply of the camp. Critical scholars assert that this list of stations, attributed in the Bible to Moses when he "wrote their places of departure according to their journeys" (Num. xxxiii. 2), was really written down by a Jewish priest during or after the Captivity, who either drew on his imagination or was singularly well informed on the subject. How it became possible for a priest in Babylon to gain such accurate knowledge of the distances and routes in the desert of Sinai—a region then unvisited by either Jews or Chaldeans—it is not easy to understand. The writer represents Edom as peopled by a rude tribe akin to the Hebrews, but with admixture of Hittite and Ishmaelite (or half-Egyptian) blood. In the days when Judah languished in Babylon, the region round Petra was held by Nabathean Arabs, who came up from the Nejed; for Gilead and Moab and Edom had been crushed much earlier by Assyria, when Tiglath Pileser III. took captive the sons of Gad and Reuben. The topography of the Exodus is an actual topography, easily followed on the ground; and the chronology of the Hebrew text of the Old Testament agrees, from Abraham's time downwards, with monumental dates. There would be nothing strange in the preservation of an original list of stations written by Moses, among a people to whom the art of writing was already known, and it may in time come to be recognised that the words of the Pentateuch form a better foundation for history than the fragments of Manetho, or the baseless theories of those who set aside its dates and its geography as fabrications of a later priesthood.

NOTES TO CHAPTER III.

Egyptian Dates.—The reign of Thothmes III., beginning about 1600 B.C., was fixed by Dr Brugsch from the notice of the rising of the star Sothis on the 28th Epiphi, or (at that period) 20th July, during his time ('Hist. Egypt,' vol. i. p. 395), checked by certain observations of the moon. The dates of the earlier dynasties are still uncertain, and the chronology of Manetho is still accepted as a rough guide, but the average of thirty years for a king's reign appears to be much too high. The early kings of Babylon (like our Saxon kings) ruled on an average only eight years. The Turin Papyrus disagrees with Manetho as to the reigns of the fourth and fifth dynasties, Suphis ruling six years (Manetho, 66), Mencheres twenty-four (Manetho, 63), and Tatcheres twenty-eight (Manetho, 44): the average for seven reigns of the fourth dynasty is only sixteen years. If the Table of Abydos is correct in giving sixty-five kings between Mena and Ahmes (or before about 1700 B.C.), an average of sixteen years' reign would bring Menes down to about 2800 B.C. The Turin Papyrus, however, gives an average of twenty-seven years for eight reigns of the twelfth dynasty, and this dynasty would have begun about 2400 B.C. The thirteenth Theban dynasty consisted of forty-seven kings according to the Turin Papyrus, but Manetho says sixty kings. The Theban and Hyksos kings were contemporary, and some of the earliest dynasties were probably rulers of only part of Egypt. The early chronology is therefore at present very imperfectly known (see 'Brugsch, 'Hist. Egypt,' vol. i. pp. 33, 67, 120, 188). The average reign of the Theban kings (thirteenth dynasty) was only seven years.

Numerals in the Old Testament.—The fact that the numerals were very liable to be miscopied is clearly shown by comparison of the versions. In addition to the changes made in the Samaritan and the Septuagint respecting the lives of the earliest patriarchs, where the corrections seem to be deliberate, there are many other instances, some of which appear to have no motive for alteration, and merely indicate a different text. Thus, for instance, in 1 Sam. xiii. 5 the Peshitto Syriac reads 3000 for 30,000 chariots, whereas in 1 Kings v. 11 the Septuagint gives 20,000 for 20 measures of oil. In 2 Kings i. 17 the Septuagint reads eighteenth for second year of Jehoram. In 2 Chron. iii. 4 the Septuagint makes the Temple 20 cubits instead of 120 in height. These are only specimens showing the alterations noticeable throughout the Bible. The early monuments make use of numeral signs instead of writing numerals in full, and to the miscopying of such signs the variations are probably due in many cases.

Kadesh and Kadesh Barnea.—The discovery by Rowlands of a fine spring called '*Ain Kadis*, in the Tih desert, has led to a controversy as to the site of Kadesh Barnea. The new site agreed well with the account of the Kadesh to which Hagar fled (Gen. xv. 14) on the way to Shur, near Egypt (verse 7, compare Gen. xx. 1). There was a Kedesh in this region (Josh. xv. 23) near Adadah (*'Ad'adeh*), but in neither case is this site stated to be the same as Kadesh Barnea or the "Holy place of the desert of Wandering." The latter is called a "city" on the extreme border of Edom (Num. xx. 16), near Mount Hor (verse 22, see xxxiii. 36, 37). It is probably the Kadesh attacked by Amraphel (Gen. xiv. 5) near Mount Seir and Paran (see Num. xiii. 26), and at the south-east corner of the Hebrew territory (Num. xxxiv. 4), eleven days' journey from Horeb "by the way of Mount Seir" (Deut. i. 2, 19); and it marks the east limit of conquest as compared with Gaza on the west (Josh. x. 41). It was east of Hezron (*Jebel Hadireh*), and near the Dead Sea (Josh. xv. 3), and Ezekiel points (xlvii. 19) to the same situation. There is no reason for discrediting the Jewish tradition, preserved in the Talmud and by Josephus, which places Kadesh Barnea at Petra close to the traditional site of Mount Hor; and this indeed is the only place—except Elath—in the desert where a "city" has ever existed.

CHAPTER IV.

HEBREW CIVILISATION.

Having thus followed the thread of history over the whole period covered by the Pentateuch story, it is necessary to consider, before treating of critical opinion, questions relating to language, writing, civilisation, natural history, and religion, which are illustrated by monumental records, and which are of the highest importance in forming an unbiassed opinion as to the character and age of the five books which formed the Torah or "Law" of Israel.

Language is one of the surest marks of date in writing. When we compare modern English with that used in the Bible three centuries ago, or again with the Anglo-Saxon whence it mainly springs, we mark the slow and constant change of speech from age to age. This change is less rapid among peoples whose literature preserves a written standard than among savage races. The Semitic languages were slow to move, and the Aramaic of Hammurapaltu differs little from that of Nebuchadnezzar. But the language of various parts of the Bible offers to our study very remarkable changes at different periods.

The study of monumental texts, though still very imperfect, because they are still so few west of the Euphrates, forms a sure basis for comparison with Bible language. The Eastern Aramaic, spoken not only in Babylon and Assyria, but commonly used throughout Canaan in the fifteenth century B.C., gives us a language at once older in character and more elaborate in grammar than the Hebrew. The tendency in all speech is to clip the words, and the pronunciation of the older dialects is marked by longer forms, as a rule, than that of the later. The Eastern Aramaic, when compared with the Hebrew of Isaiah, not only presents these longer forms, but also those ancient inflections which tend to die out of language. The three cases of the noun, for instance, which survive in Arabic but are lost in Hebrew, mark the Eastern Aramaic. In our own language the inflections of the Anglo-Saxon have been lost, just as modern Persian lacks those of the age of Darius. The voices of the verb in East Aramaic are more numerous than in Hebrew, and, generally speaking, the language which we meet earliest on the monuments presents us with a more archaic speech than that of the earliest books of the Bible.

Of pure Hebrew we can as yet judge only from one inscription—that of the Pool of Siloam, dating about 700 B.C. It is the same language used in the contemporary prophecies of Isaiah, and we thus obtain a datum for study of Hebrew. The various Phœnician texts between 600 and 200 B.C. give us a dialect closely akin

MOABITE STONE.

(From Photo lent by Palestine Exploration Fund.)

to later Hebrew, yet by no means identical. Of the languages spoken by surrounding tribes we have many examples in the later Roman times, but only two sources of knowledge which carry us back to the ninth century B.C. The Moabite Stone presents a dialect very closely akin to Hebrew, yet not the same. The Moabite language in 900 B.C. possessed a voice of the verb found in Aramaic but not in Hebrew, and the text indicates other Aramaic tendencies. Of the Western Aramaic, spoken in Syria between 800 and 750 B.C., we have precious examples in the texts of Samala, which preserve words thought to be only of late occurrence in the Bible.[1] This dialect stands between the Hebrew on the one hand and the later Aramaic of the Roman age preserved in the Targums. It is more remote from Assyrian than from Hebrew, and witnesses the common dialect of the Syrian tribes which lived nearest to the Hebrew kingdoms. Hebrew itself is not the same in all early works, but its peculiar features — most marked in the south of Palestine — do not serve to support the theory that the Hebrew ancestors came from Arabia, for Arab dialects are far closer to the Eastern Aramaic.

In this group of languages spoken from the Taurus to Yemen, and from the Tigris to the Mediterranean, we distinguish therefore three great families—the Assyrian, the Hebrew, and the Syrian. Their relative antiquity, as preserved in literature, is in this order, pure Hebrew

[1] See Quarterly Statement, Palestine Exploration Fund, January 1896.

being linguistically the most advanced in simplicity, and the most worn by time in its forms. What Hebrew became in later times we know from the language of the Mishna—written in the second century A.D.—and from certain texts on the Jerusalem tombs and Galilean synagogues. The progress of Western Aramaic we trace at Palmyra, where a dialect approaching the later Syriac was used in the Roman age, and from the contemporary texts of Bashan, Petra, and the Sinaitic desert. But sharp distinctions of speech, marking geographical boundaries, are unknown in any age or in any language. The various dialects shade off into those of neighbouring regions, and we find the Moabite of the ninth century affected by the Aramaic of the neighbouring Syrians, just as we trace eastern and western influences on Arab dialects in the east and west of Arabia. Hence in Hebrew also geographical position must be remembered, as well as date, in judging of language; and the admixture of new stocks transported by the Assyrians into Palestine also affected language in later times.

The earliest note connected with language in Genesis (xxxi. 47) contrasts the Aramaic speech of Haran with Hebrew, and the difference is supposed to have existed as early as Jacob's time. The latest refers to the mixed speech of Ashdod in Nehemiah's age (Neh. xiii. 24); but between these limits very few linguistic notes occur except the dialectic differences east and west of Jordan in the age of the Judges, to which we have a passing allusion (Judges xii. 6). It is through comparative study of the Bible itself that further knowledge is obtained.

The differences between Hebrew before and after the Captivity are clearly marked, not only in vocabulary but in grammar also. The later style, which culminates in the Hebrew of the Mishna, first appears in Malachi about 450 B.C. The appearance of Aramaic words and new constructions is still more marked in the Books of Ezra and Nehemiah, and a further decay of the pure language of Isaiah is clearly seen in Chronicles. The Hebrew of Ecclesiastes appears to be yet later, and that of Daniel latest of all. Persian words—which are common in the Mishna—stand naturally side by side with others which are Aramaic in the later Persian age. In Ezra Aramaic passages appear, and the Aramaic of Daniel approaches yet more closely to that which is known on Jewish monuments about the Christian era. The Hebrew language, though saved from extinction by the Scriptures, suffered by long contact with Aramaic-speaking peoples in Babylon, and yet more from the Western Aramaic of the Syrian tribes brought down by Sargon and his successors to colonise the lands from which the men of Israel and Judah were taken captive to the east.

When we turn from later books to those of the Pentateuch, we find throughout a pure Hebrew language like that of Isaiah. Persian words, later forms of grammar, and later Aramaic terms, are all alike absent from the Torah, and the painful research of scholars has not led to the discovery of any marked indications of late date in the language of any part of the Law. Whatever may be judged of style, the Hebrew of the Pentateuch is practically the same throughout, and presents the pure classic speech of the earlier prophets. It is impossible to find more than a very few expressions, in parts of the Torah regarded as late, which do not occur in others admitted to be early; and as regards some of these also, monumental evidence proves that they may be ancient. Thus, for instance, the terms *nasi* ("prince"), *sabaoth* ("hosts"), *mad mad* ("exceedingly"), which have by some scholars been regarded as late terms, occur on the Assyrian monuments and in Canaanite letters long before the Torah was written. Remarkable as is the eloquent style of Deuteronomy, the most characteristic terms used by its author are found also in other parts of the Pentateuch, and in the Books of Kings, in the early prophets, and in Ezekiel. Nowhere in the Pentateuch can the peculiarities of language so marked in Chronicles be discovered, nor is the language of any part that written by priests in Ezra's age. There are, on the contrary, archaisms in the Torah which, however often denied, are not the less certain marks of ancient language carefully preserved by scribes.[1] The evidence of language tends to show that all the Pentateuch existed before the corruption of the Hebrew language began during and after the Captivity in Babylon, and attests the careful preservation by later scribes of their sacred text.

When we turn to other books of which the date is

[1] See note, p. 74.

doubtful, geographical questions become important. It is remarkable that the Book of Ruth, which refers to the Moabite ancestress of David, is slightly tinged with Moabite words. The language of Job, which on the one hand compares with early prophets like Amos, on the other hand includes many terms nearer to Aramaic and Arabic. The scene is laid in the region near Petra, and the language appears to be that of a Nabathean writer of early date. The Song of Solomon, in like manner, presents peculiarities which may lead us to think that it was written by a Gileadite kinsman of the Ammonite bride. It has been suspected from the grammatical peculiarities of the song of Deborah that the dialect of Northern Palestine differed somewhat from that of Jerusalem. But when we turn to the Pentateuch, we find that the language of those parts which critics have assigned to a priest of Ezra's age resembles at latest that of Ezekiel, whose Hebrew still is pure. Honest scholars who still adhere to the modern theory of the Pentateuch, but whose knowledge of Hebrew is deep and sound, are thus forced to conclude that the language of the supposed later editor is "largely traditional"; yet it is almost impossible for any writer of a later age affecting earlier style to escape from the use of later forms and words. Of such anachronism there has not been found any clear instance in the Pentateuch. The language of later writers, such as Jeremiah and Ezekiel, is naturally influenced by their study of the Scriptures, and forms, therefore, a very weak basis for comparison. No distinction of language divides the priestly laws of the Torah from the narrative itself, and the whole Pentateuch is knit together by its uniform use of that pure Hebrew which was used alike by the authors of the Books of Joshua and Judges, Samuel and Kings, and by the prophets from Isaiah down to Ezekiel.

But if the language of the Pentateuch affords us no reason for regarding any part of it as late, it may be argued that in written form it cannot have existed early among a people who were ignorant of letters. This argument, which used to be maintained a century ago, has also fallen before the growth of monumental knowledge. It is certain that in Moses's age a knowledge of writing was widely spread in Western Asia. We have no reason to doubt that one "learned in all the knowledge of the Egyptians" would have been able himself to write, or to suppose that the Hebrews who lived so long among a writing race in Egypt were more ignorant than the contemporary petty chiefs of Canaan, all of whom had scribes beside them.

In the time of Moses there were three distinct systems of writing in use. The Egyptians not only used the hieroglyphic in monumental writing and on seals, but they used a running hand (the hieratic) with ink on papyrus scrolls. The Hittites and other Mongol tribes in Syria had their own hieroglyphic system, which was quite distinct from any other;[1] and the general character in use not only in Babylonia, Assyria, and Armenia, but also in Phœnicia and Canaan, was the cuneiform or

---

[1] See note, p. 74.

"arrow-headed" character. Letters sent to Egypt were there read by special scribes; and interpreters often accompanied the embassies from Asia. Letters so received were docketed before they were placed in the archives, these dockets being written in ink and in the hieratic character on the brick tablet, which was usually baked before it was sent. Letters from Egypt to Babylon were written also in cuneiform, and in the Babylonian language.

These facts seem to show that the alphabet had not as yet come into use in the fifteenth century B.C. The oldest alphabetic text known which can be dated with certainty is the Moabite Stone, about 900 B.C.; but the differences observable between its letters and those of the Siloam text (700 B.C.), and of the Samala inscriptions (800 B.C.), serve to show that the alphabet must have been in common use throughout Palestine and Syria at least as early as the time of David. We have an allusion to the "pen of the writer" as early as the fourteenth century B.C. (Judges v. 14), but the first notice of letters is in the time of David, when Samuel is said to have written a book and Seraiah was the court historian. In Isaiah's time the "common character" (Isa. viii. 1) is mentioned, and scrolls were used by Jeremiah, but it was still customary in Judah to use tablets as late as 600 B.C. (Hab. ii. 2).

Such indications as we possess seem to show that the Semitic alphabet first appeared in Syria, and gradually spread over all Semitic-speaking countries. It was adopted by the Greeks before 1000 B.C., and gradually superseded all hieroglyphic systems, though the cuneiform was still used as late as the Greek age in Babylon. The number of signs to be learned in Egypt amounted to 400, and in Assyria to 550 at least, while the Hittites used at least 130 emblems. The more practical Phœnicians devised a system which only needed 22 signs, by selecting some of the later Hittite forms;[1] and this system was specially fitted for Semitic languages though adopted with modifications by the Aryans. The original Syrian alphabet had also the advantage that its emblems were extremely distinct and much more easily read than the slovenly hieratic, which never attained to the condition of a pure alphabet. In later times this distinctness of form was much marred by hasty writing; and the Hebrew letters of the Greek period are often so much alike as to render reading difficult, but the Phœnicians even then retained the older forms only very slightly changed.

We are led, then, to suppose that any writings stored in the ark by Moses would have been written in a syllabic character, and very probably in cuneiform. The alphabet was a later system, which sprang up in the days of native independence, after the decay of Egyptian influence, about 1000 B.C., or some two centuries earlier. It is distinctly recorded that the Ten Commandments were written on tablets of stone, and on both sides of the tablet, in the "divine writing graven on the tablets" (Exod. xxxii. 16). The tablets of the fifteenth century B.C., written in Canaan,

[1] See note, p. 74.

COMPARATIVE PLATE OF ALPHABETS.

Value.	Moabite, 890 B.C.	Samala, 800 B.C.	Baal Lebanon, 800 B.C.	Samala, 730 B.C.	Jerusalem, 700 B.C.	Gebal, 600 B.C.	Sidon, 300 B.C.
Aleph	✢	✢	✢	✢	⊦	✗	✗
Beth	9	9	9	9	9	9	9
Gimel	∧	∧		∧	⊺	∧	∧
Daleth	◁	◁	△	◁	◁	△	△
Heh	∃	∃		∃	⊁	∃	∃
Vau	Y	4		4	ᛉ	4	4
Zain	I	I	I	Z	⟻	乙	～
Kheth	H	日	日	日	日	日	⊟
Teth		⊗		⊗			
Yod	↙	↗	↗	↗	↗	♆	⋀
Caph	⊬	⊬	⊬	⊬	⊬	⊬	4
Lamed	ℓ	ℓ	ℓ	ℓ	⌐	⌐	⌐
Mim	⅋	⅄	⅄	⅄	⅄⅄	⅄	⅄
Nun	⅄	⅄	⅄	⅄	⅄	5	5
Samech	‡	‡	‡	‡		⅍	⅍
Ain	○	○	○	○	○	○	○
Pe	⌐	⌐		⌐	⌐	⌐	⌐
Tsade	⊦	⊦	⊦	⊦	⊬	⊦	⊦
Koph	φ	φ	φ	ᛩ	ᛩ	ᛩ	ᛩ
Resh	⊲	9	9	9	9	9	9
Shin	w	w	w	w	w	ω	ω
Tau	✗	✝	✝	✝	✗	⊦	⊦

were graven on clay afterwards baked, and they are very generally written on both sides. Stone was, however, sometimes used from the earliest period for such records in Chaldea, and clay would not easily have been found in the desert. Whether this "divine writing," as contrasted with the "common character" of Isaiah's age, represented the cuneiform as contrasted with the alphabet, we can only conjecture. The Ten Commandments could easily have been written in cuneiform, on two tablets about six inches square, and these no doubt resembled the brick epistles preserved to us from the time of Moses.

But if the original Law had thus to be transcribed in later times from syllabic tablets on to alphabetic scrolls, various difficulties must have arisen. Unless the tablets were very carefully numbered their sequence would not always be certain, and the syllabic character is often difficult to render as regards the sounds, even when the meaning is clear. Thus when a sign for king is used, it may be rendered by various words, such as *sar*, *melek*, *nasi*, &c., at the will of the transcriber; and the true sound of personal names is for the same reason very often doubtful. A curious case in which uncertainty may have arisen from this cause is found in the name of Saul's son Ishbosheth, who is also called Ishbaal. If the original document transcribed was written in cuneiform, the sign for deity, which formed the second part of the name, may have been variously read by different scribes as Baal or Bosheth—the latter being a Phœnician deity called Bast, whose name occurs on an existing text. In the Pentateuch the name of Moses's father-in-law is variously given as Reuel and Jethro. It is not impossible that the reading of the original may have been doubtful.[1]

The cuneiform tablets are generally so arranged as to contain in each a complete document. In later times these were numbered, but the Canaanite letters which contain no dates are now difficult to arrange in sequence when found in large numbers. A Hebrew scribe copying out a succession of tablets would have found the same difficulty, unless they were carefully arranged in an order which was never disturbed. A disconnected narrative would naturally result from taking the tablets as they stood if the order had been lost.

Another peculiar feature of the Pentateuch might also be explained by the same considerations. In some narratives the word Elohim ("the Almighty") is used exclusively, in others the name Jehovah ("the living God"); in others, again, both names occur — rendered God and Lord in our English version. When we turn to the Canaanite letters we find that, in some cases, the word Elohim (used of the Pharaoh) is written in syllables, but in others it is represented only by the cuneiform emblem for deity. If this latter stood alone, without the syllabic spelling, the actual word would be unknown, and various transcribers might render it *Baal* or *Yehu* at will. In some cases modern scholars have long been accustomed to render one cuneiform group of signs by the sound *Malik*

[1] See note, p. 74.

or Baal, while more recent discoveries show that it should be rendered *Yehu* at least in many cases.

It is conceivable, therefore, that what has happened to the modern scholar might also have happened to some ancient scribe. Certain tablets may have contained the name Elohim fully written in syllables, others the sign for deity not so spelt. In the latter cases the pious Hebrew would naturally have transcribed this sign by the name of Jehovah ("the living God") whose servant he was; but respect for his original would prevent his altering the word when fully spelt. In yet other cases, when the writing was partly syllabic, partly emblematic, his copy in a single narrative would contain both words. In Genesis we have instances of each case — chapters in which the name Elohim alone occurs, and others with only the name Jehovah; but again episodes in which both words are used, and even combined, as Jehovah-Elohim.

The occurrence of these differences, if they are so to be explained, would show that more than one scribe was employed in writing down the Law; for it is usually the case that in cuneiform letters one scribe will shorten his labour by the use of emblems, while another, more careful to make clear his writing, uses syllables instead. But such differences do not show that the real author is distinct in each case. Ribadda, king of Gebal, wrote fifty letters to Egypt by aid of scribes, and at least four different handwritings are to be distinguished in them; but the true author, whose name heads all the letters, is the same, and the style of his expression is the same throughout.

If the true history of the earliest scrolls were as here supposed, the first scribe who copied the tablets in alphabetic letters on skins or papyri would have had before him distinct documents each complete in itself. First he placed the story of Creation, in which the name Elohim was written in full. His second tablet told the story of Eden, and the original scribe had used a sign for God which the transcriber was at liberty to render by the name Jehovah. Pursuing the rest of the narrative, it seems only necessary to suppose that a third writer on the tablets used both forms of writing, so that both Elohim and Jehovah would appear in the transcript. As a rule, the separate episodes seem to suggest separate tablets, completed by different scribes. The argument casts no light on the authorship of any such documents, but it serves to show that what has been attributed to difference of authorship may be due to difference of writing, and to the employment by the same author of two or three scribes. It seems to be certain that alphabetic writing was unknown in the age of Moses, and any documents that were preserved in the ark, and copied later by the Hebrew scribes, must of necessity have been in syllabic and emblematic writing, like that of the contemporary Canaanites, Amorites, and Hittites.

In addition to the art of writing, the Pentateuch records a considerable civilisation in the days of Moses. The ark, the tabernacle, the engraved gems on the ephod, the use of precious metals, the notice of chariots, of walled cities, and cultivated fields,—all indicate a civilised age, and a civilisation not confined to Egypt. The evidence of monuments and of existing remains shows us clearly that in the fifteenth century B.C. such civilisation did exist, not only in Chaldea but in Syria and Palestine as well. It is unnecessary to expand the subject at length, for the wealth of material proves to us that Syria, about the time of Moses, was everywhere occupied by civilised races.[1] The temples were full of treasure, with statues of ebony and gold: the cities were walled, the fields were full of wheat, barley, olive-trees, and vines. The Canaanites had chariots plated with silver and gold, and armour of bronze and iron, and battle-axes of flint. The tents of kings had pillars of gold and bronze: the art of cutting gems was known, and all the precious metals used. A gem with the name of Kurigalzu of Babylon, still preserved, belongs to this age. The expeditions of Egyptians and Babylonians were headed by the sacred arks of their gods, and precious woods adorned with metals were used in tents for the field. The great leather tent of Queen Hatasu, and her chair, are still preserved to us, and they were made long before the Exodus. Nothing that is said in the Pentateuch of civilisation in the fifteenth century B.C. betrays the state of Asia in a later age. Even the foreign spices from Arabia and Ionia, noticed in Leviticus, may then have been known, for the Akkadians had reached Egypt by sea ten centuries earlier, coasting from the Tigris

[1] See note, p. 76.

round the great peninsula; and Egyptian fleets went to Somali-land in Hatasu's time, while copper was carried in trading vessels from the Cilician coast to the Delta in the reign of Amenophis III. It is no doubt difficult to understand how Israel in the desert obtained so much gold, and found acacia-trees large enough to make from them the Tabernacle boards; but the profusion of precious metals among the Hittites and Amorites of this age is most astonishing, and the use of tents with pillars of gold is mentioned by Thothmes III.

When we turn to the natural history of the Torah, we are again able to compare it with that of Sinai and Palestine in our own times. Only two wild animals mentioned in the Bible are now extinct—the lion, which is mentioned by the later prophets, and whose bones are found in the Jordan gravels; and the *reem* or wild bull (rendered "unicorn" in our version), of which also the bones occur, and which was hunted in the Lebanon by Assyrians as late as the twelfth century B.C. The other beasts and birds, noticed in Leviticus and Deuteronomy, belong to the fauna of the Sinaitic desert, to the sea-shore, and to the Jordan valley and woods of Gilead. It is not a fauna distinctive of the land of exile, or of a later period, with which we have to deal, nor are the names those which the Assyrians gave to birds and beasts. Among the more distinctive are found (Lev. xi.; Deut. xiv.) the gull and the ostrich, the pelican and stork, the roebuck and fallow-deer, the ibex, the antelope, the bubale, and the wild sheep. Of these, the gull would not be found in Assyria; the ostrich still is found in the Syrian deserts, with the wild sheep and ibex. The bubale survives in the far east of Moab, the roebuck in the woods of Gilead, the fallow-deer on Tabor. The antelope courses over the plains, and the pelican rocks on the smooth Mediterranean. The crane and quail fly across the desert, the stork delights in the Jordan swamps. Last of all, the "coney" or hyrax is common among the rocks of Sinai and of the desert of Judah. The ibex is represented on an early Egyptian monument as brought by Asiatics from Edom. The lion in Lebanon is mentioned in the fourteenth century B.C. by an Egyptian traveller.

In the Pentateuch we find no notice of domestic fowls, which were known to the Persians, or of silk or cotton. There is no allusion even to elephants and ivory,[1] though elephants then existed in herds on the Euphrates, near Carchemish. The flax of which the priests' robes were spun was one of the oldest plants cultivated in the East: the almond was native to Palestine, with the pistachio and the spices carried with Joseph to Egypt. Mules, such as Hezekiah owned according to Sennacherib, are unnoticed in the Torah; while iron, which is mentioned, has been shown to have been known to the Egyptians by its Hebrew name before 1300 B.C., and has been found with flint and bronze in the lower strata of the mound at Lachish, together with seals of the time of the Exodus. The evidence of natural history, as noticed in the Torah, points to an age earlier than that in which domestic

[1] See note, p. 77.

fowls, cotton, and silk became known to the Hebrews through Persia; and the fauna of the Torah is that of Eastern Palestine, Sinai, and the shores of the sea.

In conclusion of this brief sketch of Hebrew civilisation, the question of religion must be noticed. The Tell Amarna tablets show us that the Canaanites worshipped Baal and Ashtoreth, Dagon and Asherah ("the grove" of our translation), with the famous Baalath of Gebal. They used the word Elohim as it is sometimes used in the Bible, as applying to kings and judges, and the Pharaoh is often called the "Sun-god" in these tablets; but, as far as can be discovered, the name of Jehovah was unknown among the Canaanites. The Moabite Stone proves to us that Istar-Chemosh was the deity of Moab about 900 B.C., and that Moabites then regarded Jehovah as the national God of Israel. Certain seals of the ninth century B.C., found at Jerusalem and elsewhere, are engraved with Hebrew names which are compounded with the sacred Yah for Jehovah. It is still more remarkable that the same name appears quite as early in Assyria, in the Aramaic form Yahu.[1] Thus it appears clear that long before the Captivity the name of Jehovah was known in Mesopotamia; and Sennacherib, and Balaam from Pethor, near the Euphrates, are both said in the Bible to have known Jehovah.

In the Book of Genesis it is stated that men began to call on the sacred name in the earliest ages (Gen. iv. 26), but as translated in our English version another pas-

---

[1] See note, p. 78.

sage seems to say that Jehovah's name was unknown to the Patriarchs (Exod. vi. 3). It is doubtful, however, whether this discrepancy should not be removed, for Hebrew grammar admits of another rendering: "Was not I known to them" by my name Jehovah? The nations surrounding Israel looked on this sacred name as indicating only a national god, and the Jerusalem seals —in contradiction of the Law—present us with the orb and wings of the Sun-god. But these belong to an age when the Torah was forgotten, and when the Prophets were lamenting idolatry in Israel. Common men continued down to Jeremiah's time to regard Jehovah as the rival of the "Queen of Heaven," and to attribute their misfortunes to neglect of the service of Ashtoreth. Only for a time under Hezekiah and Josiah [1] was idolatry suppressed; and under the early Judges all Hebrews still worshipped Baal. Yet the higher conception of Jehovah as the one true God was preserved by prophets from Samuel to Isaiah, and from Isaiah down to Jeremiah. The only reason for supposing that it may not have been known in the time of Moses lies in its abstract nature, hardly conceivable in an age of general idolatry. When, however, we turn to Egypt and find how early Amen is hymned as the one true and unknown God, of whom there was no real image, and who was the maker of all, we see that even as early as the Exodus other nations besides the Hebrews had risen to this great conception of a single Creator. To Ribadda of Gebal, the

---

[1] See note, p. 78.

pious worshipper of Baalath, Amen was only the god of Egypt. Dusratta of Mitani in Armenia invokes side by side his own deities with Amen, and prays to Ashtoreth to watch over his friend in Egypt. But the Egyptian poet who wrote the famous hymn to Amen had a truer conception of a single Creator; and in like manner Jehovah, who, to the ordinary Hebrew or to the Moabite, was only the Sun-god of Israel, is in the Pentateuch and in the Prophets the God of all the universe, the only Creator, to whom it was impious to ascribe material form.

To sum up our inquiry into Hebrew civilisation, we find that in the age of Moses the art of writing had as yet not attained to an alphabet, and that his records were most probably preserved in tablets written in cuneiform signs. That pure Hebrew may have been already spoken, differing from that of later times. That the Pentateuch shows no signs of Persian or Assyrian influence on language or civilisation: that the geography and ethnology, the natural history and chronology, are accurate and real, as referring to the earlier ages of the world, and present no signs of a later time. Finally, that the use of scribes, to set down the words dictated by king or lawgiver, may account for variations which are commonly supposed to denote independent authorship, and for repetitions which arose from the possession of duplicate tablets. The worship of Jehovah is traced back monumentally to the time of Ahab; and there is no true reason for denying that the conception of a single Creator may have been formed as early in Israel as the days of Moses.

NOTES TO CHAPTER IV.

Archaisms of Language in the Pentateuch.—These have been controverted but not explained. The pronoun *hua* is used for both masculine and feminine, "he" and "she"; the feminine *hia* only occurring eleven times in the Torah. It has been supposed that the pronoun was originally written *ha* for both genders, but this does not help to explain why this peculiarity was preserved by the scribes. It certainly distinguishes the Law from the later books, and was not a feature of later Hebrew. Gender is a very ancient characteristic of Semitic grammar, but not a primary feature of language; and the use of one form for both genders cannot but be regarded as archaic. In the same way *nar* (masculine), "a boy," is used in Genesis instead of *narah* (feminine) for a "girl." In the first chapter of Genesis the absence of the definite article (verse 28) has been remarked as a peculiarity. This also appears to be archaic, for the definite article is absent in Assyrian and on the early Phœnician monuments.

Hittite Hieroglyphics.—Although the study of this system is in its infancy, there is no longer any doubt that the system was distinctive of Syria and Southern Asia Minor, and existed as early as 1400 B.C. The latest results will be found in a paper by the present author ('Journal of the Royal Asiatic Society,' October 1893) where it is urged—(1) that the language was Mongolic and akin to the Akkadian; (2) that the system was syllabic with a few ideograms for "king," "country," &c.; (3) that the sounds of about half the emblems —which number some 130 in all—are recoverable from the Cypriote syllabary derived from the earlier forms, and in a few cases from the short bilinguals as yet known; (4) that the system was used by Hittites and other cognate tribes.

Origin of the Alphabet.—The Ionian alphabet contained letters not used in Phœnicia, and which are found in the

Cypriote syllabary. The attempt to derive the alphabet from the cuneiform has failed; and De Rougé's theory of Egyptian derivation fails to account for more than 21 letters, and neglects the Ionian letters. Pliny ('H. N.,' vii. 57) was uncertain whether the alphabet came from Assyria, Egypt, or Syria, and modern scholars have the same doubt. It is probable, however, that it is traceable to a single source, and

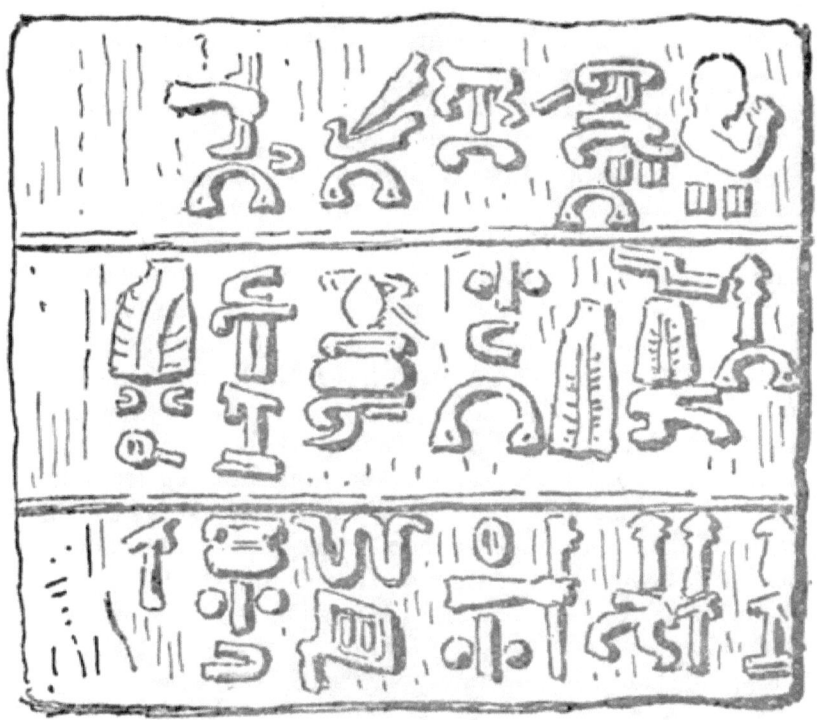

Hamath Stone, No. 1.

the Cypriote offers the closest comparison of forms, especially in the cases of the syllables *He* (for Kheth), *Wa* (Vau), *Ye* (Yod), *Ke* (Caph), *Ra* (Resh), and *Se* (Shin), as compared with the oldest Semitic types. Our information is, however, at present very imperfect. The history of the alphabet is best studied in Dr Isaac Taylor's great work on the subject, in which, though advocating the Egyptian derivation, he yet allows the possibility of an origin from the Syrian hieroglyphics.

Ideograms.—This term is used of picture emblems used to define certain classes of words in cuneiform, such as the sign for mountains or countries (originally a picture of three hill-tops), for king, for personal names of men (a vertical stroke), or of women (an emblem of the *kteis*), or of cities (an enclosure), or of gods (a star). Originally the inscriptions were entirely ideographic, but syllabic writing is known earlier than 2700 B.C. Such ideograms might be read in various ways, as more than one word existed to describe them. Instances in which various readings in the Old Testament may be due to the use of ideograms in the original records are of considerable interest, including the name Ishbosheth or Ishbaal noticed in the preceding chapter (2 Sam. ii. 10 ; 1 Chron. viii. 33), and Mephibosheth or Meribaal (1 Chron. viii. 14 ; 2 Sam. iv. 4). Jerubbaal (Judges viii. 35) becomes Jerubbesheth (2 Sam. xi. 21), and in each case the name of the deity may have been written ideographically. The Joram of 2 Sam. viii. 10 in like manner becomes Hadoram in 1 Chron. xviii. 10, probably for Hadad-ram, the name *Yo* for Jehovah being replaced by that of Hadad the Syrian god. The names of deities are very commonly ideographic in cuneiform, the sign IM standing for Addu or Hadad, and NIN for Baalath, in the Tell Amarna letters. The sign AN for the deity (originally a star) stands for Elohim in the same letters in the plural, and it is very rarely written in syllables.

Civilisation of the Canaanites.—The chief sources of knowledge are the spoil-lists of the records of Thothmes III. (see 'Hist. Egypt,' vol. i. pp. 325-353), and the Tell Amarna letters. In the former we find notice of silver, gold, gems, copper, lead, wheat, wine, incense, balm, oil, and honey ; of innumerable chariots painted and plated with metal ; of statues, tables, thrones, footstools, armour, weapons, and ploughs ; of ivory, ebony, and cedar ; of metal vessels with elaborate designs; and of horses, goats, cattle, sheep, and even apes from Asia. In the Tell Amarna texts a century later we read of merchants trading in ships from Asia Minor (Alasiya or Elishah) in copper, silver, and gold. From Babylon was sent ivory, with gold and precious woods and thrones. Balsam was also sent to Egypt. From Matiene in Armenia came copper, iron, gold, silver, and tin. The dower of Tadukhepa sent from this region included necklaces, bracelets, ear-rings, anklets, and rings; boxes of wood and vessels of bronze were sent with precious stones and cloth; chariots with harness adorned with gold lions and eagles are noticed in the same list, and horns of the wild bull. Similar presents were sent in the fifteenth century B.C. to Egypt by the Hittites. Dusratta mentions the treasures of the Temple of Baalath at Gebal; and this civilisation is traceable in all parts of Syria and Palestine.

Elephants on the Euphrates.—The fact that the range of the Asiatic elephant in early times extended to Mesopotamia seems to be established by the record of Amenenhib, an officer who, under Thothmes III., attacked one of a herd on the Euphrates near Ni or Ninus Vetus (Brugsch, 'Hist. Egypt,' vol. i. p. 354). There are also various references to ivory sent to Egypt from Asia. In the catalogue of spoils taken at Megiddo ivory is noticed, and an elephant's tooth was sent from Asebi or Cyprus. In the list of presents from Babylon (Tell Amarna letters, No. 4, British Museum collection), *biri* or ivory is also noticed. The Egyptian name for the elephant (*eb*) is apparently the same as the Hebrew *hab* and Assyrian *habba*, also the Sanscrit *ibhas*. This question is interesting in connection with Solomon's ivory throne (1 Kings x. 18); and an ivory throne of Hezekiah is noticed in Sennacherib's record. In later times, ivory was well known to the Hebrews coming from Dedan on the Persian Gulf (Isa. xxi. 13; Ezek. xxv. 11-15) and from Cyprus (Ezek. xxvii. 6), and yet earlier it came with apes from Tarshish to Solomon (1 Kings x. 22). The Coptic *eboy* preserves the Egyptian name of the elephant, and the name of the ape — Hebrew *koph*, Latin *cepus*, Sanscrit *kapi*—is also found in Egypt as *kafi*, while apes are noticed as sent to Thothmes III. from Syria ('Hist. Egypt,' vol. i. p. 521). These indications also affect the question of the situation of Tarshish (see Notes to chap. ix.)

The name of Jehovah in Assyria.—According to the Book of Genesis (iv. 26), the sacred name was known from a very early time. Baalam from Pethor on the Euphrates (Num. xxii. 5, 8) also appears as a worshipper of Jehovah; and Sennacherib claims (2 Kings xviii. 25) to come up against Judah in the name of Jehovah. According to another passage (2 Sam. viii. 10), Joram, son of Toi, king of Hamath in David's time, had a name compounded with *Yu* or Jehovah, and monumentally a king of Hamath named *Yehu-bihdi* is believed to be noticed. But the most important evidence is that collected by Mr T. G. Pinches (see 'Proceedings of the Biblical Archæological Society,' 1st November 1892), showing that a deity named *Yau* or *Yahu* was worshipped in Assyria as early as the ninth century B.C. The names *Belyahu* (Bealiah, 1 Chron. xii. 5), *Nadbiyahu* (Nadabiah), and *Nuriya* (Neriah) occur on these early texts with others. A coin of Gaza, of about the fourth century B.C. ('Journal Asiatique,' i. 83), represents *Yahu* driving in a chariot. The sacred name is, however, not found in the Tell Amarna letters of the fifteenth century B.C.

Destruction of Canaanite Idols.—The fact that the provisions of the Law were carried out in Palestine, probably by Hezekiah and Josiah, seems to be indicated by the absence of bas-reliefs and of rude stone monuments west of the Jordan. Canaanite Teraphim, or small images, have been found in the mound at Lachish. Rude stone altars and *bamoth*, or standing-stones, occur in great numbers east of Jordan, but not a single bas-relief or statue of early date has been discovered in Palestine. One such has been found at Damascus, and others in Phœnicia and in Northern Syria. Stone altars also occur at Dan near the source of Jordan, and a few remain in the wildest part of Upper Galilee; but in Judea and Samaria all such monuments appear to have been destroyed if they existed.

CHAPTER V.

THE PENTATEUCH.

The Law or Torah has always stood alone in Jewish estimation as separated from all other sacred books. It was so when Josephus wrote, and when the son of Sirach (about 200 B.C.) spoke of "the law and the prophets, and the others who followed them." It was so also when the Law was rendered into Greek (250 B.C.), and when the Samaritans accepted the Pentateuch, but adopted no other Hebrew books. The Torah is never known to have included anything beyond the five books into which it was divided later; and Jewish tradition is in this respect probably a better guide than modern theory.

The later Jews regarded all the Law as having been written by Moses, although no such assertion is found in its pages. Parts of Deuteronomy are indeed cast in the first person, and the early laws in Exodus are said to have been written by Moses himself. But it is difficult to suppose that he would have written an account of his own death; and the expression "unto this day," found frequently in the Torah, points to some lapse of time. Yet the indications of a later age are few and uncertain, for it can hardly be held that the menace of exile (Lev. xxvi. 33), with the promise of victory attached, must of necessity point to the later days of the kingdom. Invasions of Palestine began in Abraham's time, and continued in all later ages. The king of Babylon, allied by marriage to Amenophis III., threatened to invade Canaan if its inhabitants rebelled against Egypt in the fifteenth century B.C. The Assyrians came as far south as Beirut in the fifteenth and in the twelfth century; and the Assyrian king buried a century later at Abydos may have passed through Palestine.[1] The certainty of invasion must thus have been present to the minds of Hebrews as early as the time of Moses.

Several other indications of a date later than that of Moses are said to occur in Genesis. The first is the notice of Dan (Gen. xiv. 14), a place not so named till the time of the Judges. The second is the notice of Hadad or Hadar in Edom (Gen. xxxvi. 39), who is assumed to have been the contemporary of David. The third is the allusion to Shiloh (Gen. xlix. 10), also supposed to point to the age of Joshua at least. To these the reference to Rameses (Gen. xlvii. 11) may be added, since that name occurs in Egypt only in the times of the nineteenth dynasty. These, however, are but feeble indications of date. The words "unto Dan," if really referring to that town, may have been added as a gloss, as may the famous allusion to the kings of Israel (Gen. xxxvi. 31). The name Hadad was a common one among

[1] See note, p. 96.

Syrians; and the translation of the passage as to Shiloh is doubtful, and differs in various versions. The notice of Rameses is less easily explained; but none of these indications carry us down later than the time of David, when the transcription of the original Torah might be supposed to have been made. The name of Agag, mentioned by Balaam, is in like manner not of necessity that of the king conquered by Saul.

It is argued, however, by critics that the various books of the Torah contain contradictions which point to different ages in which different authors lived. The three important arguments concern the central sanctuary, the position of the Levites, and the dignity of the sons of Aaron. In Exodus "all sanctuaries" where the name of Jehovah is recorded are blessed (Exod. xx. 24); but in Deuteronomy (xii. 13) Israel is warned not to worship "in every sanctuary that thou seest," but only in the central shrine chosen out of all the tribes. On this weak foundation a critical theory rests; but it seems clear that the warning in the second case refers to Canaanite temples, while it is not clear that in the former passage several contemporary shrines are meant. The Jews have always understood this passage to refer to the various central shrines at which the ark rested. In the desert these rapidly succeeded each other as the Hebrews marched on. In Palestine various centres were established successively at Shechem, Shiloh, Kirjath-jearim, Nob, and Gibeon, before Jerusalem became the final centre. In Deuteronomy the Israelite dwelling too far off is exempted from the duty of annual pilgrimage; but in Samuel it is recorded that pious Israelites came year by year to Shiloh before the loss of the ark. Even in Joshua's time the tribes beyond Jordan showed signs of defection, and under the Judges men did what was "right in their own eyes." The central shrine was never fully re-established after the ark had been captured by the Philistines; for until David's time the tabernacle at Nob and Gibeon formed one sanctuary, while the ark at Kirjath-jearim constituted another. Only under David and Solomon was the concentration of worship really effected, for the severance of Israel from Judah at once led to the establishment of new centres at Bethel and Dan.

As regards the Levites, it is urged that in Deuteronomy they occupy a position as local priests in all the cities of Israel, but that they were afterwards concentrated at Jerusalem and given cities as property. Finally, in the latest age, it is urged that they became servants of the priests who belonged to the family of Aaron, and ceased to be priests themselves as they were in the time of Micah, according to the Book of Judges. These various differences are supposed to distinguish the age of the earliest Law, and of the author of Deuteronomy, from that later period when the supposed "Priests' Code" was written during and after the Exile.

When, however, we study closely the various passages concerned, this distinction becomes less clear. The Levitical cities are in two cases mentioned in the early history in connection with Levites—Bethshemesh in the time of Samuel (1 Sam. vi. 13-15) and Anathoth in that of Solomon (1 Kings ii. 26); but when we turn to the time of Nehemiah we find no distinct separation of Levitical cities. It would have been quite possible that the Levites, like the modern Dervishes, should have possessed property — such as is ascribed to them even in Deuteronomy—and should have also been sent as instructors in the Law to the various cities of Israel, without denying that they may also have come up yearly to Jerusalem with the rest of Israel. It is nowhere stated that these Levites acted as priests, except in the case where Micah —in an age of lawlessness—made of a Levite the priest of his idol shrine, and in the later case of certain apostate Levites, who were excluded from the Temple as having also offered heathen sacrifices in Samaritan sanctuaries. Every priest was a Levite, but every Levite was not a priest.[1] The superior dignity throughout the Torah is reserved to "Aaron the Levite," chief of the tribe, and to the descendants of his sons.

The early existence of a written Law is attested both by various passages in the Prophets and by two distinct statements in the Book of Kings. Hosea wrote about 730 B.C., and condemns Israel for neglect of the Torah: " I have written for him the great things of my Law, but they were counted as a strange thing " (Hosea viii. 12). In Isaiah, Jeremiah, Amos, and Micah similar allusions occur. The Book of Kings is believed to have been

---

[1] See note, p. 96.

written before the Captivity, and it is therein stated that King Amaziah of Judah about 820 B.C. obeyed an injunction found in Deuteronomy, which is described as "written in the Book of the Law of Moses" (2 Kings xiv. 6). But two centuries later we find (2 Kings xxii. 8) that the Law had been so utterly forgotten that its existence in the Temple was unknown. The high priest told the scribe, "I have found the book of the Law in the house of the Lord," and its discovery was followed by a new reformation. This second passage is often quoted; and Hilkiah is even charged with having imposed a recent forgery on the Jews as the original Law of Moses. But the earlier statement must be considered to have equal weight, if we attach any value to the words of the Hebrew historian.

It is equally clear that the whole thread of traditional history, and many of the special institutions noticed in the Torah, existed in the eighth century B.C. when the great prophets wrote. In their pages we find allusions to Nimrod, to Abraham, to the destruction of Sodom, to the story of Jacob's flight to Haran and his marriage, to Israel leaving Egypt and abiding forty years in the desert, to Moses, Aaron, and Miriam, to Balaam and to Balak. We also read of the Levites, the Nazarites, the ephod, the distinction of clean and unclean food, the new moons and Sabbaths, and other festivals of the Hebrews. These passing allusions do not prove the existence of all that is found in the Pentateuch, but they at least show that there is no marked difference between its contents and the conditions and traditions of the eighth century B.C.[1]

But there are other indications in later books which show that the ceremonial of the Pentateuch received additions not noticed till later. In Ezra and Nehemiah we read of the Nethinim, the singers, the porters—classes not mentioned in the Torah—and of the "wood-offering," which became an important Jewish rite, but which does not appear as an early institution in the Law. There is in the Pentateuch no allusion to a permanent temple, no notice of Jerusalem, no allusion to Tirzah or Samaria, or to the existence of a rival shrine at Bethel. Negative evidence is no doubt weak, but we might certainly have expected that later additions to the Law would have borne some reference to later conditions.

We are forced thus to ask why it is that critical opinion demands that the Torah should be regarded as consisting of many fragments of various ages, compiled and edited by a later priest, in direct disobedience of the injunction which he left standing in Deuteronomy? "What thing soever I command you, observe and do it: thou shalt not add thereto, nor diminish from it" (Deut. xii. 32). "Ye shall not add to the word that I command you, neither shall ye diminish from it" (Deut. iv. 2). These commands are preserved in passages which, according to critical theories, are by no means the latest in the Pentateuch.

The earliest observations on which critical objections

---

[1] See note, p. 97.

were raised have already been mentioned. Astruc, a Belgian doctor, to whom Voltaire alludes as wasting his time on the subject, was the first to point out the existence of supposed parallel passages in Genesis, distinguished by the use of the names Jehovah and Elohim. These two documents were regarded twenty years ago by critics as forming a double work in Genesis, and discoverable also in the later narrative of Exodus and Numbers. A third author was supposed to have added the Book of Deuteronomy, while Leviticus and parts of Exodus and Numbers, which refer to the ritual of the Hebrews, were finally separated out as a "Priests' Code" and attributed to the age of the Captivity.

The more, however, this theory was studied, the more difficulties was it seen to involve. The distinction of the two documents in Genesis proved to be far less easy than at first thought, and differences of opinion arose as to the dates of the authors. It was also found that similarities of style and language connect the early narrative with the legal chapters, and that Deuteronomy contains matter only elsewhere found in Leviticus. Neither by style, by language, nor by historic statement, could the various periods be distinguished so as to lead to general consent. The more the writers the greater the number of opinions.

It has thus resulted that the theory now maintained differs entirely in principle from that of the last generation of critical writers. An editor is supposed to have gathered together, during the Captivity, numerous documents which he somewhat clumsily strung together, taking extracts at will, and connecting them with a thread of his own writing, and even adding important chapters. The manifest unity of design in the Pentateuch is thus explained as artificial, and the whole work becomes a series of cuttings from various sources, so ill assimilated as to be divisible, and supposed to contain contradictions which the editor failed to see. Some of the chapters (such as the first of Genesis and the account of the purchase of Machpelah by Abraham) which used to be regarded as the oldest of Hebrew writings by critics, are by the younger school assigned to the editor and become the latest. Some of the criteria which used most to be urged as decisive are now abandoned, and instead of four books by four writers we are now asked to suppose that many separate fragments, some of which were composite themselves, have been loosely welded together by the later compiler.

On what basis does such a theory rest? Not on language; not on the evidence of versions; not on historic statements; not on manuscripts. The whole language of the Torah is ancient: the variations of the versions of the Law are comparatively so few and so small as to prove the careful preservation of the text from an early age; the historic statements of the Pentateuch point also to an early age and not to that of Ezra; the oldest Hebrew manuscripts hardly differ at all in any important features from the received text. The only appeal that remains is to literary style—to the critical taste of the scholar, which has differed so much in a generation that what was once regarded as oldest is now supposed to be the most recent addition. There is surely nothing which eludes the critic more than literary style. It rises and falls with its subject, and differs within the lifetime of any author. After the dry laws in Leviticus, the last chapter rises in an eloquent strain similar to that maintained throughout Deuteronomy. The Assyrian scribe in like manner will insert, in a single inscription, a poetic notice of the army's advance over rugged mountains, and a mere list of conquered tribes. A vision of a prophet of Istar interrupts the history of an Assyrian war. In all ancient Semitic writings this sudden change of subject and tendency to repetition is observable, and most of all in the Koran. But repetition is not regarded by critics as a sign of dual authorship, for they refer to one writer the most remarkable repetition in the whole Pentateuch—namely, the account of the Tabernacle and its furniture in Exodus (xxv.-xxx. and xxxv.-xl.), first as commanded and then as made.

When we examine more closely the results which are supposed to have been established, many difficulties and differences arise. The task of dividing exactly the Elohim and Jehovah documents in Genesis leads to no certain result. Critics admit that the style is not sufficiently distinct to lead to certainty, and though the writer who uses the term Jehovah is thought to be freer and more detailed in his accounts, yet the language of both is alike. In Numbers (xiii. 1-23) a double account of the journey of the spies is supposed to be traceable — the priestly editor supplying the preface with an occasional interpolation in the older account. It is argued that in one case they start from Paran, and in the other probably from Kadesh. The text says that Kadesh was in Paran (verse 26), and the only difficulty seems to be that the episode as a whole is out of proper sequence in the story. The greatest uncertainty, however, occurs when the work of the editor and the date of the " Priestly Code" come to be considered. Here we find that the list of genealogies and of places, the dry details of priestly ceremony, and other prose portions, are all allotted to this later priest. Yet he is supposed to have penned the magnificent first chapter of Genesis, and the graphic account of Abraham's dealings with the Hittites. So far, therefore, criteria of style and subject escape us: and as regards the "Priests' Code," it is admitted by critics that in some respects it appears to be earlier than Deuteronomy, but in others later, in some more elaborate and therefore later than Ezekiel, but in other passages simpler, and so— it is urged—earlier than that prophet. Thus the "Priests' Code" has again to be divided up, and the process of subdivision has now been carried so far that when interpolations, distinct sources, glosses, and other corruptions are added, many chapters read in sentences supposed to result from the additions of four or five writers composing a single clause.

The tree must be judged by its fruits, and the cardinal assumptions of the theory have produced a result which has no known parallel in actual literature. We know quite well what was the Jewish practice of later times. They were zealous to preserve the text of the Law, in obedience to the commands in Deuteronomy. They wrote Targums or paraphrases in Aramaic, and separate treatises on the observance of various laws forming the Mishnah. When this last in turn was rendered sacred by increasing antiquity, they wrote commentaries in Aramaic on its text. But we have no knowledge of a Jewish scholar mutilating the writings of his ancestors, or of his composing a book of fragments from unacknowledged sources, linked together by a few words of his own writing. That kind of book-making is characteristic rather of our own times; and no editor who so presented to us as the Law written by Moses a composite later forgery could escape the charge of literary dishonesty.

The Book of Deuteronomy stands last in the Pentateuch, and sums up the whole of the Law, including passages only found in what is called the "Priests' Code." It adds new and important material, but the attempt to show that it is at variance with what precedes is generally confined to minute differences which have small importance, and in some cases the subject considered is not the same as in another passage compared by critics. The magnificent eloquence of Deuteronomy thus seems to set the seal on what goes before, and in part it echoes the very voice of Moses; but it can hardly be doubted that the author, when speaking in the historic third person, and recording the death of Moses, lived at a somewhat later time. "No man knoweth of his sepulchre unto this day" (Deut. xxxiv. 6), are almost the last words in the Torah, which ends with praises of the great national hero, which would not have been written by so meek a man as himself.[1]

The general conclusion from such study seems to be that, while we have distinct statements which refer certain laws—including the Ten Commandments—to the hand of Moses himself, the Law as transcribed in a later age from its original tablets cannot be wholly ascribed to the first Hebrew age. Additions were no doubt made, but internal evidence does not help us to say exactly when. Samuel is recorded to have written in a book the "manner of the kingdom" (1 Sam. x. 25); and the duties of a king as laid down in Deuteronomy (xvii. 16) might well have been so described in Samuel's time. Even if we accept all the indications which have been mentioned, no historic statement carries us down later than David's time. The preparation of rolls of the Law in alphabetic writing may easily be supposed to have been undertaken when first the Temple was established in Jerusalem. Finally, as regards the various repeated narratives in the Torah, it is possible to conjecture that more than one copy of the original existed; for in Assyria this has often been found the case, various copies of one tablet having been found which, though slightly different in wording, are substantially correct. If, when the Torah was so transcribed, one of the tablets spoke of the order to make the

[1] See note, p. 98.

Tabernacle, and another of its making, it is possible that both were transcribed in order that nothing might be lost.

To endeavour exactly to follow out the process of transcription would be a hopeless task. It has led to the extraordinary and impossible division of the Torah into fragments labelled E, J, H, D_1, D_2, P_1, P_2, by critics —not including other "sources"; and the older and younger schools of critics are not agreed, and differ in principle as well as in details. Where such scholars have failed, it is not likely that others in the future will succeed. We must be content with very general results, and views held with great reserve; but the theory of a "Priests' Code" dating as late as the Captivity is one certain to be abandoned, because unsupported by cogent argument. The laws in Leviticus are often quite as archaic as those of the "Book of the Covenant" in Exodus: the allusions to Moloch worship, witches, and the scapegoat point to early times. The elaboration of ritual and wealth of priests do not of necessity point to a late age. During the Captivity all such rights were lost, and never afterwards acknowledged by the whole population of Palestine. In Egypt and in Western Asia generally there was, on the other hand, an early organisation of priests, who levied dues and received offerings and tithes. The age of Solomon is one in which the priestly organisation was perhaps more complete than in any later time; but even in Abraham's days, and yet earlier, the monuments of Chaldea record the regular establishment of dues in Akkadian temples. Why need we, therefore, seek to bring down the date of Hebrew laws concerning the sacred service or civil duties to the latest period of the ruined kingdom?[1]

If ever it should come to be generally acknowledged that transcription is the true explanation for those literary features which have been supposed to mark late date and various authorship, it will be seen that each episode, complete in itself, was probably recorded on a separate tablet. Thus in Genesis the scribe would have before him the Creation tablet standing alone, and next to it the tablet of Eden. He had two versions of the list of ancient patriarchs (Gen. iv., v.), one of which gave the length of their lives; and the fifth tablet was the story of the sons of God and daughters of men. The sixth was the Flood story, with a separate account, perhaps, of the clean beasts; the seventh was the tablet of Races; the eighth the story of Babel; and the ninth the list of Abraham's ancestors. In some of these divisions the name Jehovah is used exclusively, in others that of Elohim; but, as already urged, the difference may originally have been graphic, and due to later copying of syllabic and emblematic signs used by older scribes.

The same division into separate sections continues throughout Genesis; and the tenth tablet gave the early history of Abraham, while the twelfth is devoted to the raid by Amraphel. Two versions of the story of Hagar seem to have been copied, and this is the most remarkable

[1] See note, p. 99.

parallelism in all Genesis (Gen. xvi. and xxi.); but in one case Hagar's flight precedes the birth of Ishmael, while in the other it follows it. It is not unlikely, of course, that she should twice have fled from her mistress. There is a similar parallelism between the story of Abraham in Egypt and of Isaac at Gerar (Gen. xx. and xxvi.), yet the fraud practised by the patriarch in either case is the only real connection. There is a curious break in the history of Joseph when the episode of Tamar is introduced (Gen. xxxviii.), but this would easily be explained if Joseph's long story occupied more than one tablet of the original. As to the number of words that any tablet would contain, we have only to remember that several hundred lines are often found on tablets not more than 18 inches in length.

The same system of explanation will be found to apply equally to the rest of the Torah: it would serve to explain alike the interruptions of the text and the recurrence of one subject repeated with but little alteration. Whether it would, however, account for the summary to be found in Deuteronomy seems doubtful. The book reads rather as a general reflection on the Law as a whole by some later prophet, whose eloquence and inspiration rise with his subject. To such a prophet following Moses the book itself alludes immediately after the "manner of the kingdom" has been described (xvii., xviii.) It may be that to Samuel we should ascribe these passages which have no counterpart in the rest of the Law, and that the final transcription of the original tablets was carried out in the time of Saul and of David, or early in Solomon's reign, from those documents which had been stored in the ark, with perhaps some additions of later times.

The suggestions so made are not due to any previously formed literary theory, but are the consequence of what seems to be established by the discovery of ancient remains. If we accept the statement that there was once an ark in which laws written by Moses were stored, those tablets must have been transcribed later from syllabic characters to alphabetic, and the results would be such as have been sketched. If, on the other hand, we deny that any such documents existed, and attribute the whole of the Pentateuch narrative to the invention of later priests, we are still confronted with the results of monumental study, which serve to show that the tradition preserved in Genesis of early times was historically correct. While, on the one hand, the Rabbinical belief that all the Law was written by Moses is not supported by the Bible itself, on the other the very contrary results which have arisen from a century of critical study serve to show that the origin of the Pentateuch is still little understood, and that literary criticism by itself leads to no satisfactory solution.

NOTES TO CHAPTER V.

The Assyrians in Egypt.—The early relations between Egypt, Assyria, and Babylon in the fifteenth century B.C. are proved by the Tell Amarna texts, and an Assyrian visit to Egypt appears to have occurred as early as the time of Rameses XVI., who married the daughter of Palhaskharnes, the "great king of Assyria." A tablet in the language of Babylon was erected to "Naromath, king of kings, the great king of Assyria," who was buried at Abydos, and he appears to have been the grandfather of Shishak, who reigned 966-933 B.C. ('Hist. Egypt,' vol. ii. pp. 196-202). These notices are of interest in connection with the prophecy of Balaam (Num. xxiv. 22) speaking of Assyrian inroads, and of attacks on Assyria by the Cyprians; and also with the inroads of Cushan Rishathaim (Judges iii. 10) about 1400 B.C.; but monumental information about this time is unfortunately very imperfect.

Priests and Levites.—The position of the Levites, as being at once teachers of the Law in various cities, ministers at the central shrine, and owners of land, was exactly that of the modern Dervish orders, who possess lands and monasteries, but are scattered as teachers among the villages of Palestine, and assemble in bands at certain festivals. The antiquity of the cities assigned to Levites is monumentally proved in many instances. Gibeon and Bethhoron, for instance, occur in Shishak's list, Gezer in the Tell Amarna letters with Ajalon; Eltekeh is mentioned by Sennacherib, and Taanach by Thothmes III. with Ashtaroth.

The extreme critical theory regards the Levites as being the local priests of the Hebrews, and Aaron as a later creation of priestly tradition. Aaron is, however, called a Levite in a passage not regarded as being late (Exod. iv. 24), and is mentioned in Deuteronomy (v. 20) in evident allusion to the narrative of the golden calf (Exod. xxxiii. 5). The expression "the priests the Levites" is by no means peculiar to Deuteronomy, for it occurs in the later prophets (Isa. lxvi. 21; Ezek. xliv. 15). There is no passage in the Torah which attributes to Levites not of the family of Aaron an established situation as priests. In Deuteronomy (xviii. 6, 7) the Levites appear both as living in the various cities, as pilgrims to the central shrine, and as possessing a patrimony. In Ezekiel the idolatrous Levites are excluded from the sanctuary (xliv. 10). In Deuteronomy the priests of the tribe of Levi are noticed as teachers of the Law (xxxiii. 10). Aaron is mentioned by the prophet Micah (vi. 4) with Moses and Miriam, but in all parts of the Torah the Levites not of the family of Moses appear as ministers of the sanctuary only.

The Prophets on the Law and History of Israel.— Allusions in the prophetic books before the Captivity are of great value for critical research. The Law is distinctly noticed as "written" (Hosea viii. 12), and is often mentioned as known but neglected (Isa. ii. 3; Jer. viii. 8, ix. 13, xxvi. 4; Micah iv. 2; Zeph. iii. 4). The Sabbath is also specially noticed as a day of rest (Jer. xvii. 24. Compare Isa. i. 13; Hosea ii. 11; Ezek. xx. 12). Allusions to circumcision (Jer. ix. 25) and to Nazarites (Amos ii. 11; Lam. iv. 7) occur, and Jeremiah alludes to the setting free of Hebrew slaves (Jer. xxxiv. 9; Exod. xxi. 2). The ephod is noticed by Hosea (iii. 4), who also speaks of unclean food (ix. 4). Incense—which is monumentally noticed before the time of Moses—is also mentioned by Isaiah (i. 13; see Jer. xi. 13, xvii. 26). Hebrew festivals are also indicated (Hosea ii. 11, ix. 4, 5; Amos v. 21, viii. 10). References to the narrative of the Torah also occur—to Nimrod (Micah v. 6), to Abraham (Micah vii. 20), to Sodom, Gomorrah, Admah, and Zeboim as destroyed (Isa. i. 9; Amos iv. 11; Hosea xi. 8), to Jacob's marriage in Aram (Hosea xii. 3, 12), to Moses, Aaron, and Miriam (Micah vi. 4; see Jer. xv. 1), to the Exodus (Jer. ii. 6, xxxii. 21; Hosea xi. 1, xii. 9), to forty years in the desert (Amos ii. 10, v. 25), to Balaam, son of Beor, and to Balak (Micah vi. 5), to Oreb (Isa. x. 26), to the crime of Gibeah (Hosea x. 9), to Samuel (Jer. xv. 1), and to Shiloh (Jer. vii. 12, xxvi. 6). In the later part of

Isaiah Sarah is noticed (li. 2), and Abraham and Jacob (xli. 8, 14), as is also the passage of the Red Sea (lxiii. 11, 12). In Ezekiel there are references to Eden as the garden of God (xxviii. 13, xxxi. 8, 16, xxxvi. 35). The sin of Adam is mentioned in Job (xxxi. 33). There are, on the other hand, no allusions in the Torah, or in the prophets, to the Nethinim (1 Chron. ix. 2; Ezra ii. 43), or to the singers and porters of the Temple (1 Chron. ix. 17; Ezra ii. 41), or to the wood-offering (Neh. x. 34). The Urim and Thummim mentioned in Samuel were non-existent in Ezra's time (Ezra ii. 63).

Writings ascribed to Moses.—Certain passages of the Torah alone are directly stated to have been written by Moses himself, including the curse on Amalek (Exod. xvii. 14), and the Book of the Covenant (Exod. xx.-xxii.; see xxiv. 4, 7, 10-26), with the tablet of the Commandments (Exod. xxxii. 15), and the journeys of Israel (Num. xxxiii. 2). In Deuteronomy there are more general allusions to the Law written in a book by Moses (xxxi. 9-11, 24-26), and stored in the ark (see 1 Kings viii. 9). The song and blessing of Moses are also said to have been spoken by him (Deut. xxxi. 30, xxxiii. 1). There are, on the other hand, notes in the Book of Deuteronomy which seem to indicate later additions, such as the geography of the desert (ii. 2), the ancient populations (ii. 10, 23), the old names of Hermon (iii. 9), the account of Og's throne (iii. 11), the origin of the name Havothjair (iii. 14) "unto this day" (xxxiv. 6); while in Numbers there are allusions to early songs (xxi. 17, 18, 27-30), as well as to the "Book of the Wars of Jehovah" (xxi. 14, 15). It is not absolutely necessary to suppose that the description of the king (Deut. xvii. 14-20) must have been written after Saul's election. The writer in the Torah says, "Thou shalt say I will set a king over me like as all the nations that are about me," and in the Tell Amarna collection occurs a letter (No. 58, British Museum collection) addressed to "all the kings of Canaan," in the fifteenth century B.C. But such notes as that which speaks of the kings who ruled in Edom "before there reigned any king over the children of Israel"

(Gen. xxxvi. 31) must clearly have been added later to the category, if it was written before Saul's time.

Antiquity of Laws in Asia.—Some indications of the existence of early laws, civil and religious, are found in monuments. A fragment of an Akkadian code exists which prescribes the punishment for those who denied their obligations to father, mother, wife, or son. The wife who denied her husband was drowned, but the husband who denied his wife was only fined, so that the inferiority of women was part of the Akkadian as of every other early system. We have also the account of a boundary fixed between Babylonia and Assyria by Assur Uballid and Burnaburias in the fifteenth century B.C. Trade documents, relating to agreements before witnesses, are preserved as early as 2100 B.C., including the sale of fields. The regular payment of bequests to a temple is noticed on the statue of Gudea at Tell Loh yet earlier, and a tablet of the time of Nebuchadnezzar (in 603 B.C.) speaks of the tithes of the temple of Istar at Sippara. The treaty of Rameses II. with the Hittites, in the fourteenth century B.C., mentions the extradition of criminals, and provides (compare Deut. xxiv. 16) that the relatives of a criminal are not to be punished in his stead. The extradition of criminals seems also to be noticed in one of the Tell Amarna letters from Armenia (No. 24, British Museum collection). The Akkadian hymns (see chap. xi.) speak of laws binding on kings as sacred obligations. The antiquity of a priestly caste in Egypt who owned lands is clearly indicated on the monuments, where—as in Mesopotamia—the king was not only the head of the priesthood, but was regarded as a divine incarnation. The priestly duties of a king are indicated in Deuteronomy (xvii. 18), and these were carried out not only by David or Solomon, but even by Agrippa, as mentioned in the Mishnah. Moses is called a king in the blessing (Deut. xxxiii. 5).

CHAPTER VI.

JOSHUA.

A NEW era in the history of Israel dates from the passage of the Jordan and the conquest of Palestine. In the Bible we are told that the Hebrews first gained the mountain plateau at Ai, near Bethel, and made peace with the Hivites, who lived between Shechem and Jerusalem. They fought the Amorites at Gibeon, and pursued them into Philistia. The route then led by Lachish up the broad valley of Elah to Hebron; and Debir on the hills overlooking Beersheba was the most southern town attacked. The Canaanites of Sharon, who had chariots, were not driven out; and there is no account of any fighting in the Samaritan mountains. The second campaign was against the northern nations who gathered at Hazor in Upper Galilee; and a great victory was gained near the waters of Merom, where even the chariots failed before the Hebrew charge. It would seem that seven years were occupied in reducing Western Palestine, but many fortified towns which did not actively oppose the Hebrews were left untaken. The great raid had not the character of a complete conquest, for many years were occupied after the death of Joshua in further conflicts, and towns like Debir rose from their ashes, and withstood Caleb and other survivors of the generation following Moses. The Canaanites and Philistines in the plains remained, indeed, unconquered to the time of Solomon, and regained their independence after his death. When, in the days of the Judges, the power of Israel died out, invaders from south, north, and east pressed hard on the Hebrews in the mountains of Judah and Ephraim, and not till David's time was the ruler of Israel the master of all Palestine and of Southern Syria.

The rivalry of Judah and Joseph dated from the first days of the conquest, when these two great tribes divided Southern and Central Palestine between them; but according to the Book of Joshua a regular division of the land between twelve tribes (including the two sons of Joseph — Ephraim and Manasseh — and excluding the sacred tribe of Levi) was made after the victory of Hazor, and the geographical chapters of Joshua are the fullest in the Bible. It is remarkable that during the wars of Joshua's age we find no allusion to any conflict with the Hittites. They lived in his age in Northern Syria, and are not mentioned at Hebron. This, as has been already shown, agrees with the historic fact that the Hittites had been defeated at Megiddo a century earlier by Thothmes III., and driven northwards. It is only in the earlier age of Abraham that their occupation of the Hebron mountains is noticed. In the Tell Amarna correspondence no single letter attributable to a Hittite exists which shows their presence in the south. The Canaanite princes of that region seem to have been all Arameans—Amorites and Philistines—owing allegiance to Egypt. The attack of Hittites on Damascus and Bashan is mentioned; and a Hittite prince of Reseph, north of Tadmor in Syria, wrote one letter to Egypt in the fifteenth century B.C., penned in his own non-Semitic language. The power of the Hittites in the north had been broken by Dusratta of Armenia before the time of the Hebrew conquest, and their raid on Damascus, during the period of the great rebellion, led perhaps to no permanent result. The greatest conquering tribe among the Canaanites was the Amorite nation, which was purely Aramean. In Syria they extended their victories as far south as Tyre. They also occupied the Jerusalem mountains and those of Hebron. East of Jordan they had conquered Moab before the approach of Israel, and had divided the whole country between Dibon and Hermon into two equal kingdoms, under Og of Bashan and Sihon of Heshbon.

The monumental notices of the Abiri are of the highest interest in studying the history of the Hebrew conquest about 1480 B.C. They occur in the letters sent to Egypt by the Amorite king of Jerusalem. They show that the Abiri came from Seir, and fought at Ajalon; that they invaded the Philistine plains, and destroyed all the Canaanite rulers. These notices agree exactly with the Bible account of Joshua's first campaign; and although the only name mentioned as belonging to one of their leaders is not noticed in the Book of Joshua, it is still a well-known Hebrew name (Elimelech) which belonged to a descendant of Caleb in Bethlehem (Ruth i. 2) in the days of the Judges.

The principal passages in the Jerusalem letters clearly indicate the path of conquest, and the terror of Canaanite

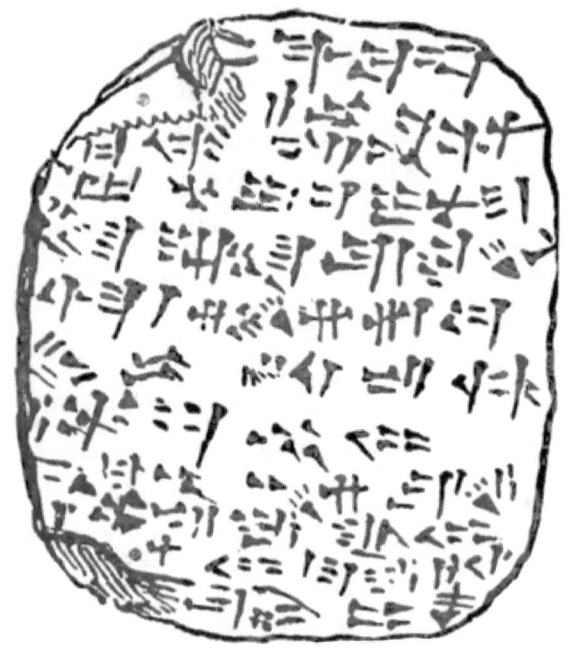

Lachish Tablet.
(Front.)

princes. The Amorite in various passages writes as follows:—

"I ask the resident of the King my Lord why dost thou tremble before the Abiri." "They have destroyed all the rulers. There is no ruler now, O King my Lord." "The Abiri chiefs plunder all the King's lands, since the

Egyptian soldiers have gone quitting the lands this year." "The King's land rebels to the chiefs of the Abiri." "Lo! the land of Gezer, and the land of Ascalon, and the land of Lachish, they have taken to themselves — this tribe who have caused the destruction of the town of Ajalon." "They have fought against me from the land of Seir to

Lachish Tablet.
(Back.)

the city of Gibeah of Carmel." "Lo! the land of Labaya and of Shaalbim is inhabited by the Abiri chiefs." He alludes also probably to the taking of Shiloh and Rimmon north of Ai, and very clearly to the conquest of Lachish. He makes preparation for leaving Jerusalem; and one letter on a different kind of clay seems to have been written after his flight, while on the way to Gaza. According to the Book of Joshua the king of Jerusalem was captured at Makkedah near Ekron, after the defeat of the Amorite league at Ajalon. Nor is it only this king who mentions the Abiri, for Princess Basmath, widow of the king of Gezer, describes her flight to Zabuba in Lower Galilee, and speaks of the attack made by these conquerors on Zoreah near Gezer. It is also remarkable that the name of one of the princes writing from Gezer is Japhia, which (Josh. x. 3) is stated in the Bible to have been that of the Amorite king of Lachish. Two fragmentary letters from Hazor also form part of the Tell Amarna collection, written by a chief whose name may read *Yebaenu* or Jabin. These likewise refer to a powerful attack by enemies whose name is not given, and ask for aid from Egypt.

It appears, therefore, that the Abiri conquest was not a mere local rising. It was the invasion of a people from the "land of the Abiri," who came from Seir, and who destroyed all the rulers, and apparently wrecked the Canaanite temples. They refused to give tribute, and swept over all the country of Judah as far as Carmel south of Hebron. That they did not meet Egyptian troops seems clear from the repeated complaint of the king of Jerusalem as to the withdrawal of the Egyptian garrison. The tone of all the Canaanite letters is a despairing cry for help to Egypt, but none of them record that any help was sent, though eagerly expected. They relate no victories over the Abiri, and the history of the reign of Amenophis IV.

shows us only defeat and disaster. In the Book of Joshua there is no account of any fighting in Central Palestine—the Hivite region,—and it is remarkable that none of the Canaanite letters come from this region. There is a gap between Megiddo and Accho to the north, and Joppa, Ascalon, and Jerusalem on the south. It may perhaps be explained by supposing that the Hebrew treaty with the Hivites gave to them peaceful possession of the country round Shechem; for, if the chapter relating to the great ceremony at Shechem stands in its proper place in the Hebrew text, this ceremony took place after the first campaign, but before the great battle near Hazor in the Amorite region of Upper Galilee.

The text of the Book of Joshua does not appear to have been preserved by the Jews with that scrupulous care which marks their veneration of the earlier Pentateuch. In the Greek Septuagint translation the order of the chapters is changed, and a whole verse is added to the lists of cities in Judah—a gloss which seems to be of late date, since it does not agree with the account of the border of Benjamin. The language of the book is very similar to that of the Pentateuch, and many passages are in the eloquent style of Deuteronomy. It consists of two parts—the first relating the conquest of Palestine, the second describing the lots of the tribes, and ending with the burial of Joshua. The geographical chapters are attributed by recent writers to the same priestly editor of later times whose work is supposed to be found in the Law. It is important, therefore, to examine this geography, and to ask whether it bears evidence of late date, and agrees with the condition of Palestine under the Persians.

The Book of Joshua is not said to have been written by that great soldier. It contains an ancient extract from the Book of Jasher concerning the miracle of Gibeon, which is related solely on the authority of that early song. The Book of Jasher, as is clear from another passage (2 Sam. i. 18), contained also songs of the time of David, and the natural conclusion would be that the Book of Joshua, as at present existing, was not earlier than David's age, and was written five centuries after the conquest. It contains the tradition of two great miracles, that of Gibeon taken from an older source (Josh. x. 13), and that of the passage of Jordan. It is remarkable that a stoppage of the river is historically stated, by an Arab author,[1] to have recurred in the thirteenth century A.D., when Bibars the Egyptian conqueror was building the Damieh bridge over Jordan. The marshy banks of the river, in a part of its course which is narrow, were undermined by the floods and dammed the stream for several hours, leaving the river-bed dry below the dam. Not only is this recorded, but the scene of the stoppage is the same as in the Book of Joshua; for the Damieh ford is the probable site of the "city Adam" where Jordan, swelled by the melting snows of Hermon in April, "rose up on a heap very far off, by the city" (Josh. iii. 16).

[1] See Quarterly Statement, Palestine Exploration Fund, July 1895.

But if the notice of the Book of Jasher points to the later age of David, other indications seem to show that the narrative of Joshua cannot have been written much later. It is difficult to believe that a Jewish writer of later times would willingly have admitted that the first centre of worship for Israel was at Shechem, and this applies to the author of Deuteronomy as well as to the writer of the Book of Joshua. In Deuteronomy Joseph and Judah are equally blessed, as also in the song of Jacob. The latter bears marks of being yet more ancient, for Levi is not a sacred tribe in Jacob's song, whereas in Deuteronomy they appear as teachers of the Law, and ministers of the altar (Deut. xxxiii. 10). The language of the Hebrew prophets regarding Ephraim is very different to that of the earlier books, and Gilgal, which in the Book of Joshua is a sacred centre, was to them an idolatrous shrine. In Samuel's time it was still a sacred place where justice was administered, and only in the eighth century B.C. is it first noticed with disfavour.

The mention of Jerusalem by the author of the Book of Joshua has been thought to mark a later age. The letters now discovered prove, however, beyond dispute, that the city was so named as early as Joshua's time. There is no allusion in this book to Jerusalem as a sacred centre, or to any temple there established. It appears as the home of Jebusite and Amorite, and as a city fighting against Israel. In the geographical portion we read that "the Jebusites dwell with the children of Judah at Jerusalem until this day" (Josh. xv. 63), a condition which existed in David's time, but which is unnoticed afterwards, and not applicable to the time of Ezra.

The geographical chapters are most clearly explained by aid of the long list of 119 towns conquered by Thothmes III. in Palestine before the Exodus. We thus are able to prove that many of them were standing long before the Hebrew conquest. Others are mentioned in the Canaanite letters as already detailed. On the other hand, several towns noticed in the Book of Nehemiah are not found in that of Joshua. Tirzah in Samaria is noticed (Josh. xii. 24), but Samaria itself is not mentioned. No mark of late date is therefore discoverable in the names of the cities.

As regards the boundaries of the tribes, it is to be noted that those of Judah and of Benjamin are much more minutely described than the rest, although in every case the account is sufficient to allow of border lines being laid down on the map with great exactitude. The information regarding western Manasseh is especially defective, and very few Samaritan towns except Shechem, Tirzah, and Tappuah, with the torrent of Kanah, are noticed. The author distinguishes the hills of Judah from those of Israel (Josh. xi. 21), and claims the cities of Philistia for Judah, though in the narrative we have no account of the conquest of Gaza, Ascalon, or Joppa. On the other hand, in the first section of the book we find the Philistines still unconquered (Josh. xiii. 2-6), with many places in the north, and the whole of Syria to Gebal and Hamath.

These regions were subdued by David, and the author clearly refers to a former age.

The twelve tribal lots agree closely with the twelve provinces into which Palestine was divided under Solomon (1 Kings iv. 7-18), but they do not accord with later divisions of the country. In Ezra's age the tribe of Benjamin occupied Lydda, which in the time of Joshua belonged to Dan, and Judah occupied towns which are given in the earlier book to Simeon. The topography of Joshua's division does not even accord with conditions existing in David's age, for Simeon is stated by a later writer to have been then dispersed, apparently migrating to Moab from the plains of Beersheba (1 Chron. iv. 31). In Hezekiah's time they conquered Mount Seir, and dwelt there down to the times of the Greek dominion (verse 43). The Moabite Stone speaks of "men of Gad" in cities which are given to Reuben in the geography of Joshua. The Gadites were taken captive in 734 B.C. by the Assyrians, with Reuben and Manasseh (1 Chron. v. 26), on the occasion of Tiglath Pileser's raid on Edom; and yet earlier the same conqueror invaded Galilee (2 Kings xv. 29) and took all the land of Naphtali, Galilee, and Gilead. The topography of the Book of Joshua is a real topography, penned by an author to whom the neighbourhood of Jerusalem was familiar, but who had also general knowledge of the whole of Palestine. It is not the topography of later times, while its accuracy forbids us to suppose that it can have been written down in Assyria by a priest who had never been in Palestine. The

Levitical cities bear, in many cases, very ancient names, and were inhabited by priests and Levites—as already explained—in at least two cases, as early as the times of Samuel and Solomon. There is no discord between the geography of the narrative and of the geographical chapters, and no evidence of late date in either, but, on the contrary, much that only applies to an age earlier than that of Solomon.

The natural result of such inquiry seems therefore to be, that while the story of the conquest may have been written five centuries after the events, and drew from ancient songs of the Hebrews the account of miracles like those at Gibeon and Jordan; and while the twelve tribes represent a condition of Israel still existing in Solomon's age, but not in that of Ahab, a century later, —yet the tradition was true, and the line of Joshua's first campaign exactly that recorded for us by the Amorite king of Jerusalem, whom he conquered. Respect for boundaries was a peculiar feature of Semitic civilisation even earlier than Joshua's time. We find the early kings of Babylon and Assyria laying down a boundary between their dominions before the Exodus. Dusratta the Armenian, in Joshua's age, has described for us the borders of his conquests from the Hittites from Haran westwards. The Book of Deuteronomy inculcates respect for landmarks, such as were set up between fields in Chaldea long before the days of Moses. It is quite possible that the borders of the tribes, still preserved under Solomon, may have been established at the time of Joshua's conquest. In that account we have both the original line separating Judah and Joseph, and also its later modification when lots were given to Benjamin and to Dan.[1] A priestly editor in Ezra's age would have been apt to describe Benjamin's possessions as existing in his own time; and the Danites in Judges desert their original home to wander north to Hermon. On no book of the Bible has recent exploration cast more light than on that relating the story of the Hebrew conquest of Canaan.

[1] See note, p. 114.

NOTES TO CHAPTER VI.

Topography of the Book of Joshua.—The recovery of about 160 cities unknown previously, which is due to the Survey of Palestine, has led to a much better understanding of the topography of this book. The boundaries of the tribes can be laid down with great certitude (see Conder's 'Handbook to the Bible'). The lot of Judah ran on the south to Petra, and thence to Hezron (*Jebel Hadireh*), and to the *Wâdy el 'Arish.* On the north from the Jordan mouth, by Beth Hoglah (*'Ain Hajlah*), it passed to Gilgal (*Tell Jiljûlich*), to Adummim (*Tal'at ed Dumm*), and to En Rogel (*'Ain Umm ed Deraj*): following the Hinnom valley south of Jerusalem, it reached Nephtoah (*'Ain 'Atân*), south-west of Bethlehem, and by Kirjath-jearim (*'Erma*) and Chesalon (*Kesla*), it entered the plain at Bethshemesh (*'Ain Shemes*) and Timnah (*Tibneh*), going north to Ekron (*'Akir*) and to Jabneel (*Yebnah*) on the sea-coast (Josh. xv.) The original border of Joseph (Josh. xvi.) ran from Jericho (*'Ain es Sultân*) to Bethel (*Beitin*), Archi (*'Ain 'Arîk*), and Ataroth Adar (*ed Darieh*), and by the lower Bethhoron (*Beit 'Aûr et Tahta*) to Gezer (*Tell Jezar*) and the sea. The north border of Ephraim ran from Ataroth Adar and Bethhoron the upper (*Beit 'Aûr el Foka*), by the valley of Kanah (*Wady Kanah*), to the plain east of Shechem, and by Taanath Shiloh (*Ta'na*) and Janohah (*Yanûn*) to Jericho. After the final division of the country the north border of Benjamin is described, coinciding with that of Ephraim to Bethhoron, where it turned south to Kirjath-jearim (*'Erma*) and Nephtoah (*'Ain 'Atân*), Rachel's tomb being on this border (Josh. xviii.; 1 Sam. x. 2). Gezer, which was not occupied by Joseph (Josh. xvi. 10), thus fell within the border of Dan, which (Josh. xix. 40) included Zoreah (*Sur'ah*), Eshtaol (*Eshu'a*), Ir Shemesh (*'Ain Shemes*), Ajalon (*Yalo*), Thimnathah (*Tibneh*), Ekron (*'Akir*), Gibbethon (*Kibbieh*), Jehud (*El Yehudiyeh*), Bene Berak (*Ibn Ibrak*), Rakkon (*Tell er Rakkeit*), and the coast east of Japho (*Yâfa*), the exact line on the north being unstated. Manasseh appears to have claimed Northern Sharon and Carmel. Issachar held the plains of Lower Galilee, and the towns of Jezreel (*Zer'in*), Chesulloth (*Iksâl*), Shunem (*Sâlem*), Haphraim (*el Ferriyeh*), Shihon (*'Ayûn Sh'ain*), Anaharath (*en N'aûrah*), Rabbith (*Râba*), Remeth (*Râmeh*), Engannim (*Jenîn*), and others. The south border of Zebulon is described from Daberath (*Debûrieh*), by Sadid (*Tell Shadûd*) and Japhia (*Yâfa*), to Jokneam (*Tell Keimun*) : on the north, by Gittah Hepher (*el Mesh-hed*) and Rimmon (*Rummâneh*), it passed to Hannathon (*Kefr 'Anân*) and to Dabbasheth (*Tell Dabsheh*), and thence west to Cabul (*Kabûl*) and Beth Dagon (*Tell D'auk*) : the shore of the bay north of Carmel seems to have belonged to Zebulon, though the expression "to Carmel seaward" (Josh. xix. 26), as belonging to Asher, is difficult to understand. The lot of Asher, from the vicinity of Accho along the shores to Sidon, included the cities Achshaph (*el Yâsif*), Hammon (*'Ain Hamûl*), and Kanah (*Kanah*), with Tyre (*es Sûr*). Naphtali occupied the mountains of Upper Galilee, and the plateau west of the Sea of Galilee, including the towns of Adami (*ed Dâmieh*), Nekeb (*Seiyâdeh*), Jabneel (*Yemma*), Hukkok (*Yakûk*), Hammath (*Hammâm Tabariyeh*), Adamah (*Admeh*), Ramah (*Rameh*), Hazor (*Jebel Hadîreh*), Kedesh (*Kedes*), Edrei (*Y'ater*), En Hazor (*Hazîreh*), Iron (*Yarûn*), Migdalel (*Mujeidil*), and Beth Anath (*'Ainatha*). The lot of Simeon, on the extreme south, was carved out of that of Judah, including Beersheba (*Bir es Seb'a*), Sharuhen (*Tell esh Sheri'ah*), En Rimmon (*Umm er Rumamîn*), with other doubtful towns. Beyond Jordan the tribe of Reuben occupied the country east of the Dead Sea, from Aroer (*'Ar'air*) on the Arnon, by Medeba (*Mâdebeh*) to Heshbon (*Hesbân*), and farther south Dibon (*Dhibân*) and Beth-baal-meon (*Tell M'ain*) : on the west limits were Kirjathaim (*el Kureiyât*), Sibmah (*Sâmieh*), and Beth Jeshimoth (*Suweimeh*)—see Josh. xiii. 15-20. The tribe of Gad held the country from Heshbon northwards as far east as Rabbath Ammon (*'Ammân*), and Mahanaim (*el Mukhmah*)—Betonim (Josh. xiii. 26) being perhaps the *Butein* district in North Gilead. In the Jordan valley their towns included Beth

Aram (*Tell Râmeh*), Beth Nimrah (*Tell Nimrîn*), Succoth (*Tell Der'ala*), and Zaphon (probably *'Amâteh,* in the north-west of Gilead), or all the western slopes of Mount Gilead. Manasseh occupied Bashan and the eastern part of Gilead, with the towns of Ashtaroth (*Tell 'Ashterah*) and Edrei (*edh Dhr'a*), Mahanaim (*Mukhmah*) being on the extreme south-west border (Josh. xiii. 29-31). These boundaries, proposed by the present author in 1879, will be found on most recent maps, and they differ considerably from those proposed by writers who studied the subject before the survey of Palestine had been undertaken.

CHAPTER VII.

JUDGES.

The history of the Book of Judges carries us from the death of Joshua to the time of Eli, and covers 370 years—for Samson is clearly stated to have judged, in the "days of the Philistines," who oppressed Israel for forty years (Judges xiii. 1, xv. 20). We are thus carried from the conquest to about the year 1100 B.C. The book resembles in style and language that of Joshua, but was clearly written after the establishment of the kingdom. It includes, however, in the song of Deborah, a Hebrew ode probably as old as the fourteenth century B.C.

The period of the Judges was one of weakness and confusion, when the worship of Canaanite gods was common among the Hebrews, and when they were oppressed by Aramean, Midianite, and Philistine rulers. The episodes which it contains relate to all parts of Palestine, but do not form an exhaustive history of the whole country. The various heroes who arose in various tribes, and who for a time asserted the old supremacy of Israel, are noticed in historic order, but some episodes are only dated by the sequence of the story.

The period is one also of which as yet we have no continued monumental history. A great gap occurs in the history of Assyria before the twelfth century B.C.; and the latest Tell Amarna letters only bring us down to the time of Horus, when Assur Uballid, the ruler of Assyria, re-established relations with Egypt. It was perhaps in his reign that Chushan-rishathaim, king of Mesopotamia, invaded Palestine and enslaved the Hebrews for eight years after the death of Caleb. After this period the nineteenth dynasty arose in Egypt about 1400 B.C., and King Seti began his attack on the south of Palestine, penetrating to Kanana close to Hebron—now the ruined site Kan'aan.

A very valuable indication of early Assyrian inroads into Palestine has quite recently been recovered ('Journal of the Royal Asiatic Society,' October 1894), showing that Assur Uballid—the same Assyrian ruler who wrote one of the letters of the Tell Amarna collection—attacked Beirût about 1400 B.C. He had made peace with Babylon, and established a boundary line between the two kingdoms, but was subsequently involved in war with Cassite invaders, whom he conquered at Babylon. A rising of all the peoples, "from sunrise to sunset," occurred during his reign, and the Assyrian army "besieged the city Beirût near the land of the Amorites." The walls appear to have been undermined, and the people were taken into captivity. This account is interesting in connection with that in Judges of the eight years' servitude of the Hebrews under Chushan-rishathaim of Mesopotamia about the same period (Judges iii. 8), and with the allusions in the Law to Assyrian captivity (Num. xxiv. 22; Lev. xxvi. 32-44).

The famous Rameses II. commenced his conquests by the capture of Ascalon about 1325 B.C. or later.[1] He entered Galilee and besieged Tabor and towns in the mountains near Kadesh Naphtali. According to the Bible chronology, Jabin II., king of Hazor, lived in this same age, and was supported by a *sar* of the army, with a chariot force stationed at Harosheth, north of Carmel. The word *sar*, which is uncommon in the early books, is often found in the Tell Amarna texts as meaning a "chief." The name of Sisera does not appear to be Semitic, but is easily explained as Egyptian — *Ses-Ra* being the "child of Ra" the Sun-god. The coincidence seems to show that the old conditions of the fifteenth century B.C. were re-established by Rameses II. after his conquest of Upper Galilee, and that an Egyptian general with a force of chariots was left to secure the fealty of the king of Hazor. This would explain why Sisera, in the song of Deborah, appears as leader of several "kings of Canaan," not merely as the native general subject to Jabin of Hazor.

The conquests of Rameses II. were carried northwards to the Hittite country, and Kadesh on the Orontes fell after a stubborn battle. The Egyptians then advanced to Tennib and along the shores of Cilicia, even as far as Ephesus, but we have no account of any attempt to pene-

---

[1] See note, p. 125.

trate into the mountains of Israel. There is no mention of Shechem or Jerusalem, or of any of the cities in the hills of Southern Palestine, as attacked by Rameses II. After his conquest of the independent Hittites in the north, a famous treaty was made which granted to them equal rights as allies; and Rameses married the daughter of Kheta Sar, the Hittite king of Kadesh.

The attack on Asia Minor led, however, to reprisals, and after the death of Rameses II. the Aryan tribes, about 1300 B.C., descended to the borders of Egypt and attacked the unfortunate Mineptah, as already mentioned. A second and more terrible inroad was made a century later, in the time of Rameses III.; and the *Pulesta*, represented on his monuments as joining the invaders, are thought to have been Philistines, who also first appear as a growing power about 1200 B.C. in the Bible (Judges x. 6).

There is no discrepancy between the account in Judges and that in Joshua as regards geography. The tribes occupy the same positions in both books. Thus Benjamin and Judah (Judges i. 8, 21) alike attacked Jerusalem after Joshua's death, but failed to root out the Jebusites. Jerusalem was on the border of these two tribes. The position assigned to Joseph, Manasseh, Ephraim, Zebulon, Asher, Naphtali, and Dan is the same in both accounts. The Danites, however, are recorded to have left their proper lot near Zoreah and migrated to the Hermon valleys. Zebulon occupies the country near Tabor in Barak's time, just as in the Book of Joshua; and in the song of Deborah the neighbouring tribe of Issachar is noticed, as well as Dan and Asher on the sea-shores, farther off from the scene of battle.

The history of Gideon is not illustrated by any monumental notices, but the goddess Asherah (Judges vi. 28) is known to have been worshipped by the Amorites in Lebanon long before his time. The topography of his victory can be traced with great precision, from Bethshittah in the valley of Jezreel to Succoth east of Jordan, and north of the Jabbok, and to Jogbehah on the borders of the desert near the summit of the hills of Gilead.

No further notice is found in the Book of Judges of any attack by the Assyrians or Egyptians, and no monumental notices exist of victories in Syria after the reign of Rameses II. Under Mineptah the power of Egypt rapidly decayed, and a period of weakness and internal dissension occurred in Assyria. About 1150 B.C. Assurrisisi came as far south as Beirût, in the time of Jephthah; and in 1120 Tiglath Pileser was attacking the Hittites, and advanced as far as the sea-shore near Arvad, but none of these expeditions seem to have penetrated into the country of the Hebrews.

An interesting account is left us of the travels of an Egyptian in Palestine in the later years of Rameses II., when Egypt was at peace with the Hittites, and Galilee and Philistia gave tribute.[1] This traveller passed by Tyre to Accho, and across the plains of Lower Galilee in his chariot, and reached the "land of waters," and Tarichæae south of the Sea of Galilee. Thence he went

[1] Chabas, Voyage d'un Egyptien.

on to "the fords of Jordan," and to Megiddo, and across the plains and low hills to Joppa. He speaks of the interior of Lower Galilee as a lawless region, where he was in danger from various enemies, and where apparently the Egyptian power was not recognised. But from Joppa to Gaza he passed through the Philistine plains without any adventures. His account thus confirms what has already been said of the partial character of the second Egyptian conquest. It supplements what we learn of Hebrew history in the Book of Judges, but is in no ways discordant with the conditions of the age of Barak and Sisera.

The story of Jephthah is an episode of Mount Gilead, as that of Samson belongs to the low hills east of Philistia. In each case the topography is easily followed on the ground, and agrees with that of the Book of Joshua, but no monumental notices are known for comparison. The episode of the "sin of Gibeah," which occupies the last chapters, is one of the most remarkable, and appears to refer to the same Levite who became an idolatrous priest in Mount Ephraim. It might be thought a recent addition on account of one allusion to the "captivity of the land" (Judges xviii. 30), but the ancient manuscript of St Petersburg resolves this doubt, for it contains the reading "captivity of the ark," referring to the days of Eli. The "sin of Gibeah" is, moreover, incidentally mentioned by Hosea (ix. 9, x. 9) early in the eighth century B.C., when the story contained in Judges seems to have been already known.

During this period the Law and the worship of Jehovah were very generally disregarded, though Samson was a Nazarite, and other judges worshipped the Lord in local shrines not allowed by Deuteronomy. The statement that the Levite was "of the family of Judah," and lived at Bethlehem, is difficult to understand (Judges xvii. 7); but intermarriage between the tribes of Levi and Judah may account for the relationship; and that Bethlehem was not a city of the Levites has little importance, since they were distributed in all the cities of Israel as teachers of the Law, according to the Book of Deuteronomy.

The period of the Judges was one when men "did that which was right in their own eyes"; and non-observance of the Law in such an age does not prove its non-existence any more than the loss of the Torah in Josiah's time shows that it was not hidden in the Temple. The central shrine at Shiloh continued to exist from the time of Joshua down to that of the latest judges, and we read of a feast of Jehovah still yearly observed there, with dances in the vineyards (Judges xxi. 19). But the ark was brought out in time of war to other cities, and is found at Bethel, where Israel assembled (Judges xx. 26) to offer burnt-offerings and peace-offerings to Jehovah in a time of penitence, before the attack on Benjamin in Geba immediately to the south. The tablets placed in the ark by Moses according to the Pentateuch — two tablets of stone—were still there, according to the author of the Book of Kings (viii. 9), when Solomon placed it in the Temple; and the remaining tablets of the Law may have been likewise preserved in the Temple at Shiloh, which grew up, apparently, round the Tabernacle before the time of Eli. Yet the position of Shiloh is considered to require special description in the age of the Judges, as though forgotten by the men of Benjamin. The Levite travelling from Bethlehem, and passing by Jerusalem, "a city of strangers" (Judges xix. 12), is said in the Hebrew text to have been on his way to the "house of Jehovah" (verse 18), though the Greek translators read "to my own house." A pilgrimage to the central shrine at Shiloh seems thus to be supposed, even earlier than the days of Eli.

The natural impression which we thus obtain in reading the Book of Judges is that a period of decay succeeded that of Joshua's conquest, when the Law was forgotten and the tribes gradually grew estranged, when there was no central power, and when only the few visited the central shrine: yet when the worship of Jehovah, and some at least of the Hebrew ceremonies and customs, were preserved till Samuel arose. The monumental notices so far agree with this narrative as to show a period of confusion and weakness, of partial conquests and barbarian invasion, preceding the rise of a strong independent kingdom under David, during a time when Egypt and Assyria were both decaying Powers.

NOTE TO CHAPTER VII.

Conquests of Rameses II.—The conquests of Seti I. and Rameses II. are described by Brugsch ('Hist. Egypt,' vol. ii. pp. 10-15 and 44-75). The former king attacked Kanana (*Tell Kanā'an*), near Hebron; he afterwards penetrated to Kadesh of the Amorites (now Kades, a ruined town on the Orontes). Rameses II. stormed Ascalon, and in his eighth year (about 1325 B.C.) he took Shalama, Maroma, Ain Anamim, and Dapur, with Kalopu, and Beith Antha in the land of the Amorites. These towns seem to represent Shunem, Shimron, Merom, Tabor, Beth Anath, and possibly Shalabun in Galilee. Advancing to Beirût (where he erected a statue at the Dog river), he crossed the Lebanon, and attacked the Hittites of Kadesh and Aleppo; and after capturing the southern capital he fought against Tunep (Tennib) in North Syria, and followed the coast of Asia Minor to Ephesus. In the thirty-fourth year of his long reign (about 1300 B.C.) he married the daughter of Kheta Sar, the Hittite prince of Kadesh. The celebrated treaty with the Hittites is fully discussed by Chabas ('Voyage d'un Egyptien'), and throws light on their religion and civilisation. Since the great revolt under Edugama they had remained independent of Egypt, and the alliance was concluded on equal terms. The Hittites remained allies of Mineptah, who had perhaps a Hittite mother. Traces of the presence of Rameses II. are found in inscriptions still extant in Palestine and Syria, including that at the Dog river north of Beirût.) Another *stela* has been found near Gebal; and a *graffito* bearing his name is said to occur on the "stone of Job" in the Hauran, indicating his advance on Damascus. There is also a fragment at Arvad, found by Renan; and another, quite recently found, is said to come from Sidon ('Proceedings of the Society of Biblical Archæology,' December 1894).

CHAPTER VIII.

SAMUEL AND DAVID.

The two Books of Samuel close the older history of the Hebrews with the account of the establishment of the independent kingdom of David, extending over all Palestine and Southern Syria. In style, they have much in common with Deuteronomy, and with the Books of Joshua and Judges: they are even more graphic and more full of human interest. They contain very little of the marvellous element, excepting the voice that spoke to the child Samuel, and the visit of Saul to the witch. They cannot have been penned very long after the time of the latest events described, though the allusion to Ziklag, which "pertaineth to the kings of Judah unto this day" (1 Sam. xxvii. 6), if it be not a note added by a late scribe, points to a time when Philistia had regained its independence, and when Israel and Judah had separate kings—perhaps to the reign of Rehoboam.

The text of these two books does not appear to have been as carefully preserved as that of the Pentateuch. The Greek translation of the Septuagint contains several very remarkable omissions, whether intentional or due to a defective manuscript is not certain. That the manuscript used was written in the later Hebrew character seems probable, from the occasional confusion of the letters *d* and *r*, which is seen by comparison of the Greek and Hebrew; and it is also clear that no points were used in the Hebrew. Thus the Greek reading Edom for the Hebrew Aram ("Syria") gives us both these indications; and the Greek appears to be the more correct in this case, since the "Valley of Salt" was probably near the Dead Sea (2 Sam. viii. 13), while in another case Hadadezer and Hadarezer are both given in the Hebrew—the first being probably the true name (2 Sam. viii. 5, x. 19).

A very important difference occurs between the versions in the case of "Kadesh of the Hittites" (2 Sam. xxiv. 6), where four MSS. of the Septuagint agree against the Hebrew "Tahtim Hodshi," and clearly preserve the true reading. In the Hebrew manuscript in this case we see that the letters *Heh* and *Koph* were indistinctly written. The confusion could not occur in the earlier character, but is easily made in the later letters used in the Greek age. In several other cases the Greek reading of proper names, such as Gath, Tebah, and Edom, is the best; but in others the readings Dan and Rephaim are less correct. There is occasionally a difference in numerals—a thousand in the Greek for a hundred in the Hebrew (2 Sam. viii. 4), and four for forty in a case in which the Greek is clearly right as compared with another passage (2 Sam. xiii. 38, xv. 7).

The additions in the Greek text are as noticeable as the omissions. The words "and all the tithes of his land"

(1 Sam. i. 21) may have been added by a later priest, but in other cases no motive for the additional words is to be noticed, and the Greek translators would seem to have had before them a fuller Hebrew version. The old Syriac version also sometimes supports the Greek. There is, in short, no early book in the Bible in which the differences of the versions are as numerous and important as they are in the Books of Samuel.

The picture of Hebrew life during the century when Eli, Samuel, Saul, and David ruled, is of the highest value for comparison with that found in the Pentateuch. It shows us a nation gradually emerging from anarchy, and establishing the worship of Jehovah once more. The Law in some cases seems to be ignored; but this was generally the case under the Judges, and it gives no evidence of the non-existence of that Law.

The central sanctuary is shown to us as established still at Shiloh, and visited by the pious; but the Tabernacle is replaced by a more permanent structure with doors (1 Sam. iii. 3, 15). The boiled flesh of sacrifices (Deut. xviii. 3; Lev. viii. 31) still furnished the priests' due, but was wrongfully chosen by the arrogant sons of Eli (1 Sam. ii. 13). The Levites are mentioned (1 Sam. vi. 15) at a Levitical city; and there is allusion to Moses and Aaron (1 Sam. xii. 6, 8) as bringing Israel from Egypt, as well as to the whole thread of the history down to Samuel's time (verses 9-11). The more usual name for the deity is Elohim, and in one case the Greek uses that name where the Hebrew reads Jehovah (1 Sam. xix. 9).

On the other hand, some of the acts described do not accord with the Law. The eating of the shewbread (1 Sam. xxi. 4) was a deed of dire necessity, and the story shows us that this offering was already held sacred. This may, indeed, have served as a pretext for Saul's massacre of the priests at Nob. But it is remarkable that teraphim were still used, as in Jacob's time, by Hebrew women (xix. 13); and the sacrifices of Samuel at various shrines can only be explained as due to the destruction of the central sanctuary, or to its distance from the places named — Gilgal, Bethlehem, Kirjath-jearim, &c. The law of Deuteronomy as to hanging offenders was observed by Joshua, but not in David's time (Deut. xxi. 23; Josh. x. 26; 2 Sam. xxi. 10); but in the latter case the Gibeonites, who were Hivites, could not perhaps be expected to conform to the Hebrew custom. It is more difficult to understand how David's sons could have been priests (2 Sam. viii. 18), for though the term is rendered "chief rulers," it is that generally used of priests. That David himself should have filled priestly functions (2 Sam. vi. 13, 17, 18), if indeed we are to understand that he himself sacrificed, is less remarkable; for down to the time of Agrippa, the king — whose duty it was to write a copy of the Law (Deut. xvii. 18) — was allowed to take part in the service of the Temple. In David's time the privilege seems to have been extended to all the king's sons.

Indications of early date are not wanting in various passages. The statement that the new family of priests, which superseded that of Eli, should walk before the king "for ever" (1 Sam. ii. 35) could not have been written after the time of Nebuchadnezzar, and Solomon's throne was not established "for ever" (2 Sam. vii. 13), or even "for a great while to come" (verse 19). The psalm attributed to David (2 Sam. xxiii. 5) clearly looks forward to a long-continued rule of Israel by David's children, even if we omit the words "for all time" found in the Greek. The translation of this verse in the English is faulty, and the true rendering gives a clearer meaning. "For is not my house so [just] before God, that he hath made with me an everlasting covenant, ordered for all time and sure? for all my salvation and all my desire will not he make it grow?"

The critical views as to the Book of Samuel, which regard it as equally fragmentary and overgrown by later additions with the Pentateuch, are curiously ill supported. It is admitted that, as a rule, the narratives "point forward and backward to one another, and are in other ways so connected together as to show that they are the work of one writer"; yet this is said "not to be the case in all," and certain passages are asserted to contain a double narrative by different writers. The three earlier cases brought forward refer to the choice of Saul as king, to his relations with David when young, and to the adventures of both in the south of Judah. A double account of the Philistine battle near Jezreel is also asserted to be traceable in part. The reasons for such statements require to be carefully studied, as they affect our general views on Hebrew literary growth.

In the first instance, two independent accounts are asserted to be traceable. In the older, Saul's success against Nahash the Ammonite is held to have led—after his nomination by Samuel—to his coronation by the people at Gilgal. The later story is supposed to be at discord, and to begin with the request of the people for a king, and the election of Saul by lot at Mizpeh. In the older tale Samuel is supposed to show no reluctance, in the later he treats the request of the people with disfavour. The statement that the kingdom was "renewed" at Gilgal is regarded as the editor's attempt to harmonise the two accounts.

It is hard to see how any scholar who reads the story with care, and who remembers the tone of Hebrew thought concerning the dealings of God with man, can have reached such a result. The whole story of the choice of Saul reads continuously from point to point. The son of Kish, leaving his home at Gibeah, wanders in search of the asses of his father through Mount Ephraim and the land of Benjamin until he reaches an unknown city, probably Kirjath-jearim. Here he is chosen by Samuel by command of God, and given signs of the prophet's mission. Samuel's early reluctance to give up his power as judge over Israel (1 Sam. viii. 6) yielded to the direct command to hearken to the voice of the people (verse 9), though he delivers the protest as directed, and describes the "manner of the kingdom" (verse 9), which he also wrote in a book (x. 16, 25). From Kirjath-jearim Saul follows the valley of Sorek to the watershed near Rachel's tomb on the border of Benjamin, and thence returns to Geba, or Gibeah of the Elohim, where was his home under a Philistine ruler. The "matter of the kingdom" was, however, kept secret (x. 16), and all that Saul reveals to his uncle is Samuel's reply to his question whether the asses had been meantime found. The two chapters (viii., x.) thus refer to each other, and the divine choice remained a secret, as in the later case of the anointing of David. The Hebrews were then invited to choose a king by lot; but such lots, in other cases in the book, are always supposed to have been guided by God, who had in Saul secretly appointed the king so revealed to the people at Mizpeh. The Hebrews, though they shouted "God save the king," thought little of the unproven leader. They scoffed at him as inspired (x. 12) in popular proverbs, and the worthless despised him and brought him no presents (verse 27): all which he patiently endured.

The first proof of kingly powers was given by Saul when Jabesh Gilead was saved from the Ammonite tyrant (xi.); and the party opposing the chosen king became powerless against him, and were treated with mercy (verse 12). Samuel then invited the people to "renew" or "confirm" the kingdom at Gilgal (verse 14), and the original protest was repeated. It is hardly possible to suppose that any later writer, in times when the family of David had long been established, would have recorded this change of system, from the government by Judges to a hereditary kingdom, with the suspicion shown in the account of the founding of the monarchy. But it is easy to understand that the failure of Saul was so regarded by the early historian of David or of Solomon. The narrative bears no clear marks of double origin: the chapters refer to one another in such a manner as to link them together, and style and language are the same throughout.

Turning to the second case, we find it asserted that there is again a double story to be traced. It is said that in one David is of "mature age" (1 Sam. xvi. 14-23), brought to Saul as a harper, and made his squire. In the second account he is "a shepherd lad inexperienced in warfare," who first is made known to Saul by his victory over the giant (xvii.-xviii. 5). In the first story Saul is told who David's father was (xvi. 14-23), and knew him well. In the second (xvii. 55-58) he is obliged to ask David his father's name. It is remarkable that the Greek version omits this latter passage, as well as several that follow in the next chapter; but this appears to have little bearing on the question, and to show a defective manuscript used by the translators.

When we examine the story with care it appears that some of these critical statements are quite unfounded, and that others raise unnecessary difficulties. David was the youngest of the family of Jesse—a shepherd (1 Sam. xvi. 11) whose age is not stated, but no mere child when Samuel chose him king (verse 13). Saul's servants spoke of David as a "man of war, prudent in matters" (verse 18), but not as one of "mature age." A shepherd among the wild tribes of the desert near Bethlehem had needs be a "valiant man," and may have had early experience of fighting. No mere boy would have been able to confront the lion and the bear (xvii. 34), but David's age is not given in any part of the story. That Saul was told the name of David's father, and that David became a favourite servant, is stated (xvi. 21); and it was perhaps for this very reason that he found easy access later to the king, who showed his favour again in lending him armour (xvii. 38). Saul contrasts the age of Goliah with that of David (verse 33), but speaks of David not as a boy but as a "youth"—a term of no great precision. David speaks to the king not as a stranger first brought before him (verse 32); and though neither Saul nor Abner could remember his father's name (verse 55), it does not follow that they had not heard it. Royal remembrance of favourites is not always very lasting, and amid State affairs a king may not always recall the name of even a favourite's father. The evils of system are notable in the gratuitous attempt to split up the Book of Samuel after the same fashion as the Pentateuch—according to the latest "modern theory" of its growth.

The third case needs no special study: it is admitted to be weakly supported, and the various adventures (1 Sam. xxiv. and xxvi.) have nothing in common except the bearing of David to his enemy. The last case, however, requires special notice, because recent critical assertions are here even more misleading. Two stories are said to be distinguishable. In one case (chap. xxviii.)

the story of the witch of Endor is believed to represent the Philistines with David gathered in Shunem, and the episode is said to interrupt the story, which places the Philistines at "Aphek in Sharon," and Israel near Jezreel —David leaving the invaders before their advance. It is to be specially noticed that critics thus assume that Aphek (xxix. 1) was in Sharon, though there were there other towns so named—Aphek in Asher (Josh. xix. 30), Aphek east of the Sea of Galilee (Josh. xiii. 4), and Aphek in the Lebanon. The name, which means "the stream," was common; and it is not only not stated that the Aphek of this passage was in Sharon, but it is quite clear that it was not. What reason would Saul have had for gathering in the far north of the kingdom near Jezreel an army to oppose the Philistines gathering far south near Gath, where Aphek of Sharon (Josh. xv. 53) lay? How is such a theory to be reconciled with the words that David "returned into the land of the Philistines" (2 Sam. xxix. 11) if he really left them in Philistia itself? Ziklag, south of Beersheba, was not farther than three days' distance from Jezreel for men mounted on swift dromedaries (xxx. 1), and the Amalekites no doubt waited to attack until the Philistine army had gone to the north. It is by no means certain that the Hebrew *Ha Aphek* is to be taken as the name of a town. It means "the stream," and may well apply to that which gushes out at Shunem itself, and still waters the gardens of the village opposite to Jezreel. We cannot but conclude that the critical theorist is perversely determined to carry on the same view of double narrative which fails in three preceding cases, and that the words of the text are carelessly considered. The story of the witch of Endor stands in its natural place, after Saul's arrival in the north at Jezreel, within a few miles distance, and before the closing scene of his defeat and death. The departure of David just before the battle, and his return to Philistia, agree with the inroad of the Amalekites on the unprotected town of Ziklag. Expressions like the oath "As the Lord liveth" (xxviii. 10, xxix. 6), which are selected by critics as characteristic of this book, are not confined to either of the two supposed narratives, and often show close connection in style between the books of Samuel and of Judges. Critical views are apt to be adopted on the authority of great scholars, by those who do not study for themselves questions of geography all-important to the subject, or who disregard the beliefs of the age, and think of the Hebrews as acting from such motives as might influence ourselves.

The story of David and Solomon is as yet not illustrated by any monumental discovery.[1] No remains of Solomon's Temple have survived its rebuilding by Herod; and neither Egyptians nor Assyrians had any victories to record in Palestine during the greatest age of Hebrew power. The first monumental account of victories, after the time of Rameses II., is that of Shishak's attack on

[1] See note, p. 141.

Jerusalem when Solomon was dead. The 2d Book of Samuel is at present our only source of knowledge for David's reign. From it we gather that the capital was first placed at Hebron, in a region where David was already well known and had many friends. Saul's heir reigned in Gilead (2 Sam. ii. 8-10), and was recognised by every tribe but Judah. The first contest was waged in the country of Benjamin (verses 24, 25) at Gibeon, and the victories of David's nephews gradually established his power. After seven years and a half Israel submitted, and Jerusalem was conquered and became the central capital. The united nation turned its arms against the Philistines, who were driven back to their plains; and the ark was brought from Kirjath-jearim to the new "city of David." The building of a temple was already proposed; and the victories of David not only took the "control of the people" from the Philistines, but extended his sway over Moab, Damascus, and Edom. The king of Hamath, in North Syria, sent presents like those which had been sent five centuries earlier to Egypt, and the new family of priests faithful to David succeeded that of Eli. Even the Ammonite capital fell, after the insolence of Hanun had led to war with a people who had been peaceful under Nahash (2 Sam. x. 2), and in spite of Syrian aid from near Damascus.

Court intrigues for the succession, and the rebellion of Absolom, embittered the later years of Israel's first great king. He fled to the old capital of Saul's house at

Mahanaim in Southern Gilead. The faithful guards from Philistia, men who came from Keratiya near Gath, but who—like Obed Edom of Gath—may still have been Hebrews, followed their master with the Pelethites and Gittites (2 Sam. xv. 18), but the ark and the Levites were left in the capital. The decisive battle was fought in oak-woods south of Mahanaim, which still flourish on the slopes of Gilead; and David's power was once more established over Israel and Judah, though the rivalry which led to later separation already existed (xix. 43), as indeed it had survived from Joshua's time. Rebellion in Galilee was put down by Joab, but famine and pestilence followed the wars. The Philistines once more fought round Gath, but David, growing old, was not allowed to lead his army. The gradual growth of order and system is shown by Joab's census, which extended all over the kingdom to the borders of the allied kings of Tyre and Hamath. The north boundary of David's time reached from south of Kadesh on the Orontes to Dan-jaan on the Mediterranean south of Tyre (2 Sam. xxiv. 6). The site of the Temple was chosen, but the author tells us that only a tabernacle had as yet been commanded for Israel (vii. 6). The first treasures of the new sanctuary were warlike spoils and presents from Syria (viii. 11); and immediately after the conquest of Jerusalem Hiram of Tyre sent cedars, carpenters, and masons to build a palace for David (2 Sam. v. 11). The kingdom was secured in an age when no great rival empire in Egypt or in Assyria had power to crush Hebrew liberty, and by a man who knew the secret of all authority, as recorded in his own words (2 Sam. xxiii. 3) :—

> "He that ruleth over men justly,
> Ruling in the fear of God,
> Is as the light of morn at sunrise,
> A morn without a cloud,
> With green grass from out of earth,
> And flowers after rain."

The close of the Books of Samuel marks a period in Hebrew literature, and the end of the earlier chronicles of the history of Israel. The Book of Kings, as now existing, dates from four centuries later, and the gap is only filled by Isaiah and the prophets preceding Ezekiel. We have so far considered history, religion, civilisation, and language, down to the reigns of David and Solomon; and we have found no reason to doubt that the history is real, or that the Law existed in the earliest ages of Joshua and the Judges, however little regarded by Israel at large. We see that it is probably to ancient scribes, in the days of Samuel, David, and Solomon, that we must attribute the first transcription of the earlier tablets on rolls written in alphabetic letters, together with the history of Israel from the conquest to the first years of Solomon's reign. The Pentateuch itself clearly contains passages at least later than the times of Moses, to whom, however, the Law itself is ascribed. The mutilation of such records by a later compiler is not found to be proven by any evidence of language or of teaching.

NOTE TO CHAPTER VIII.

Topography of the Books of Samuel.—This topography has been illustrated by the exploration of Palestine, and the discovery of newly found sites. Among the more important instances are the recovery of Kirjath-jearim (*'Erma*) close to Bethshemesh (1 Sam. vi. 19, 20), and of Gilgal (*Tell Jiljûlieh*) east of Jericho. Bezek (1 Sam. xi. 8) is found at *Ibzik*, north-east of Shechem and opposite Jabesh Gilead—a place distinct from the southern Bezek (*Bezkah*) noticed in Judges (i. 4). Ramah of Samuel is probably *er Râm*, close to Gibeah of Saul (*Jeba'*), although the "Ramathites of the Zuphite clan" are noticed as living in "Mount Ephraim" (1 Sam. i. 1)—a term of vague application. The site of the contest of David and Goliah in the valley of Terebinths is indicated by the position of Shochoh (*Shuweikeh*, 1 Sam. xvii. 1), and Gath appears to be fixed at *Tell es Sâfi* at the mouth of the same valley by an allusion in the Tell Amarna letters, while Ekron (*'Akir*) lay to the west near the same valley (verse 52). Adullam is fixed at *'Aid el Mia* immediately east of Shochoh (1 Sam. xxii. 1), and a cave still exists by the ruins. Hareth and Keilah (*Kharâs* and *Kileh*) are on the east slopes of the same valley (xxii. 5, xxiii. 1), whence David retreated south of Hebron to Ziph (*Tell Zif*) and Maon (*Tell Ma'în*), and to the Jeshimon or desert west of the Dead Sea (xxiii. 14, 24, 29) at Engedi (*'Ain Jidy*). Carmel (*Kurmul*) was close to Maon (xxv. 2). The Aphek or "stream" in Shunem (xxviii. 4, xxix. 1) is immediately opposite the spring of Jezreel, which lay on Mount Gilboa. The site of the well Sirah (*'Ain Sârah*) is immediately north of Hebron (2 Sam. iii. 26). Baal Hazor (xiii. 23) is the lofty summit of *Tell 'Asûr* in Mount Ephraim. The Cherethites (xv. 18), a people often mentioned in connection with Philistia, appear to have inhabited the town of *Keratîya* in that region. Mahanaim is at no great distance (at *Mukhmah*) from one of the chief oak-woods of Gilead (xviii. 9): finally, the site of Kadesh of the Hittites (the true reading in 2 Sam. xxiv. 6 for Tahtim Hodshi) was discovered by the present writer in 1881, at *Kedes*, a mound on the Orontes south of Emesa, in a position, between the river and the tributary stream to the west, which exactly answers to the representation of this city at the Ramesseum.

The exactitude of this topography shows the intimate acquaintance of the author of the Book of Samuel with all parts of Palestine, from Gath to Rabbath Ammon, and from Ziklag to Kadesh on the Orontes; and the wanderings of David on the Philistine border, and in the extreme south of Saul's dominions, can now be traced by aid of the new discoveries of places like Adullam, Hareth, &c., not previously known.

CHAPTER IX.

KINGS.

The Book of Kings was written four centuries after Solomon's time, and is believed to date in Jeremiah's age, if indeed it was not written by Jeremiah himself. The latest date mentioned is 562 B.C. The author tells us that his materials included two ancient chronicles of the kings of Israel and of Judah, to which he refers us for further details. He also repeats the historic chapters concerning Hezekiah's reign which are found in Isaiah. He further adds accounts of Elijah, Elisha, and other prophets, but does not state his authority, and these may have been preserved only by oral tradition for the three centuries between their lifetime and that of the author. Their style differs from that of the Royal Chronicles, and agrees with the author's own style in other parts. According to the Greek translation (1 Kings viii. 12), a "Book of Odes" contained Solomon's song at the opening of the Temple, and this is thought to represent the Book of Jasher, already mentioned as being at least as late as the time of David. It is to be noted that in this chapter and elsewhere the author gives the names of the months,

Ethanim, Bul, and Zif (1 Kings vi. 1, 38), according to the ancient Hebrew calendar, which the Phœnicians continued to use till the Greek age. So also in Exodus the old name of the month Abib appears. After the Captivity these months were called by their Assyrian names, Nisan for Abib, Iyar for Zif, Marchesvan for Bul, Tisri for Ethanim. In the Pentateuch Abib stands alone without explanation, as though well known, but in Kings it is thought needful by the author to explain what month of the year is meant. The Assyrian calendar differed from that of the Hebrews, and came, no doubt, into use after the destruction of the kingdom by Nebuchadnezzar. The author of Kings found in the older chronicles the native month names, and this slight indication serves to show us the reality of his reference to older sources.

In Chronicles we have a much later account of the kingdom, by an author who carries down the history six generations later than Zerubbabel (1 Chron. iii. 21) if rightly understood. That he was a priest well versed in the Law, in the earlier books of Joshua and Judges, and in the history of the kings of Judah and Israel, is clear; but the Hebrew of Chronicles is a later language which contains many features not found in earlier books. Some of the words he uses are early known in Assyrian, but the syntax of his sentences resembles that of Esther, Ezra, and other later books, while the singers and porters to whom he refers are not mentioned as distinct classes before the Captivity. There can be little doubt that Chronicles is a book written in the Greek age, or in the last days of Persian domination, as a summary of the history of the Hebrews. The author cites his authorities for the times of the Kings, and other ancient documents (1 Chron. iv. 22) now lost to us perhaps for ever. The "Book of the Kings of Israel and Judah," whence he seems to have drawn his facts, contained, however, passages not found in the existing Book of Kings (1 Chron. ix. 1; 2 Chron. xxvii. 7, xxxiii. 18, xxxvi. 8), and either another work, or a manuscript fuller than that now known, seems clearly to be meant. The words of Samuel, Nathan, and Gad quoted as authorities (1 Chron. xxix. 29) may perhaps be found in the Book of Samuel. The words of Iddo, Shemaiah, Jehu, and Hozai may have been known to the author of the Book of Kings, who does not, however, quote such authority. A register of the tribe of Gad seems to have been made in the days of Jotham and Jeroboam II. (1 Chron. v. 17), and known to the author of Chronicles. There is no reason for suspecting historic statements merely because they are not found in the earlier history, unless they conflict with known facts; but when we compare the Book of Joshua with the lists in Chronicles, we see that defective or obscure manuscripts were sometimes used by the later scribe. The descendants of Jehoiachin are traced down later than the date at which the Book of Kings closes. The history of the dispersion of Simeon is peculiar to Chronicles. The genealogies of families after the return to Jerusalem are given by the chronicler. Many of David's heroes are noticed (1 Chron. xi. 41-xiv. 22) who

K

are not noticed in Samuel; but they belong to towns like Carmel, Gibeah, Azmaveth, Anathoth, Gederah, Haruph, &c., which were all in the south, in Benjamin and Judah, and no improbability is noticed. The source of his calculation of David's army (1 Chron. xii. 23-40) is not stated by the chronicler, nor is that of the list of Levites (xv. 1-24), or of the longer lists of Levites, gate-keepers, treasurers, generals, princes, and ministers, in Solomon's time (xxiii.-xxvii.) From the chronicler only we learn that the Tabernacle was set up at Gibeon (2 Chron. i. 3-6, 13), and that Solomon made a second census (ii. 17), and an altar of bronze (iv. 1). He speaks of the cloud and fire in the Temple, and adds words to Solomon's prayer (v. 13, 14, vi. 40-42, vii. 6), and gives us Solomon's dream (vii. 12-22) more fully. He adds Hamath to Solomon's kingdom (2 Chron. viii. 3, 4), where the older account (1 Kings ix. 18) speaks only of Tadmor or Palmyra, to the south-east of Hamath. For Solomon's reign, however, he quotes authorities not noticed in the Book of Kings.

In the reign of Rehoboam the chronicler gives us a valuable list of the frontier fortresses on the low hills west and south of Jerusalem (2 Chron. xi. 5, 12). He quotes the prophet Iddo for the victory of Abijah, which carried his frontier northwards to Bethel and Jeshanah from the earlier border of the Michmash valley, thus recovering the whole country of Benjamin (2 Chron. xiii. 19). He records (xiv. 6-15) Asa's victory at Mareshah over Zerah the Ethiopian, and his dealings with Azariah and Hanani the prophets. He speaks of the prosperity of Jehoshaphat (xvii.), and of the presents brought to him by Philistines and Arabs, as also of his victory over the Moabites near Tekoa (xx.), and quotes Hanani as his authority (verse 34). He states that Jehoram killed his brothers when he acceded (xxi. 2-4), and relates the stoning of a prophet in the time of Joash (xxiv. 14-22). Again, he mentions an army of Israelites hired by Amaziah (xxv. 5-17), and gives us a full account of the attack on Edom. The successes of Uzziah against the Philistines and Ammonites (xxvi. 5-15), and the defence of Jerusalem by engines of war, we learn only from the later chronicle; but the texts of Sennacherib inform us that such engines were in use a century later. Nor is it improbable that Jotham should have fortified Jerusalem and conquered Ammon (xxvii. 3-7), or that the Philistines in the time of Ahaz should have overrun the low hills of Judah and Dan (xxviii. 18, 19).

In Hezekiah's reign the chronicler speaks more fully of the great aqueduct made to control the water-supply of Jerusalem (xxxii. 2-8, 24-33), which still exists, and contains an inscription of Hezekiah's age.[1] He also details the new fortifications of Manasseh (xxxiii. 11-19), after his return from captivity under the Assyrians in Babylon. The captivity of Manasseh and his restoration are not noticed in the Book of Kings (2 Kings xxi.), but it is known that Babylon was subject to Assyria in his time.

It cannot be said that any of these passages in

[1] See note, p. 158.

Chronicles are suspicious, from a historic point of view. Some, like the account of the frontier fortresses and of the great aqueduct, are easily understood by the light of modern exploration. The chronicler records victories, but he also records defeats. No motive can be traced for falsifying history, and many lost books seem to have been at his disposal.

The story of the four centuries between David and Nebuchadnezzar is thus—like that of the conquest—only preserved to us in works written much later. But the authors drew their facts from tablets or scrolls preserved in the archives of Jerusalem and Samaria; and the truth of their history is abundantly proved by the archives of Sennacherib, and of other Assyrian and Babylonian kings from the eighth century B.C. down to Nebuchadnezzar's reign. It is only as concerns the stories of Elijah and Elisha that we fail to trace the author's authority. It is notable, therefore, that Hebrew chroniclers were not accustomed to ignore their sources in writing history, but quoted them by name both before and after the Captivity, as the author of Joshua also quotes the Book of Jasher, and the Pentateuch itself refers to ancient songs of Israel.

The dates contained in the Book of Kings do not always accord with one another.[1] They seem to have suffered either at the hands of copyists or in transcription from the original records. Such difficulties as to numbers meet us throughout the Bible, and the versions prove

[1] See note, p. 158.

that the copying was often imperfect. But there is nothing fabulous in any statement as to the lengths of lives or reigns in the period considered; and, generally speaking, there is not more than ten years' difference between the modern calculation of Bible dates and the modern calculation of those noticed in Assyrian records. The supposed notice of Ahab is abandoned, yet the Moabite Stone shows us that he had reigned in the period mentioned in the Bible. Ahabu of Sirlai in Syria was once hastily assumed to be Ahab of Israel; but this is impossible, and the first king who actually met the Assyrians appears to have been Jehu of Israel.

The history of Palestine after the death of Solomon can be reconstructed from the monumental records without reference to the Bible. But it presents no historical discrepancy with the Bible account, and serves to show the accuracy of the Hebrew records. Shishak has left us his list of 133 cities taken from Rehoboam in Lower Galilee, Philistia, and the mountains round Jerusalem about 965 B.C. The last name is the mutilated *Iura* . . . which is thought to represent Jerusalem itself. Among the more certainly identified names of other cities in the list are Rabbith, Taanach, Shunem, Rehob, and Haphraim in Galilee, with Gibeon, Beth Horon, Ajalon, Makkedah, Jehud, Shochoh, Ekron, Eglon, and Aroer in the mountains of Judea and in the plains of Philistia. Mesha, king of Moab, has described for us, in the ninth century B.C., his victories over Israel (2 Kings iii. 4-27) in accord with the Bible account. He recovered in Ahab's time the cities of Moab which had been subject to Omri, who is mentioned in this famous text, and he records the destruction of altars to Jehovah and the triumph of the Moabite god Istar-Chemosh.

The balance of power in the west of Asia was most complete in Solomon's age. His rule extended over all Palestine to the borders of Egypt; and by marriage he was allied to the Pharaohs, who relinquished Gezer as the dower of his bride. On the north he held Damascus, and extended his conquests to the Euphrates, founding a caravan depot at Tadmor or Palmyra, which still retains its native name in the bilingual texts of the Roman age. Solomon was allied to the Phœnicians of Tyre and to the Hittite princes of North Syria. He held Eastern Palestine as far south as Elath on the Red Sea, and married princesses from among the Ammonites, Moabites, and Hittites. The power of the Hebrews, then trading with Yemen on the south and with Tarshish [1] (or Tarsus) in Asia Minor, reached its zenith under the only king after David whose rule extended over all the country. After his death not only was the kingdom divided and invaded by Shishak, but a strong Syrian state arose at Damascus which warred for many years against Israel.

In the tenth century B.C. Asa sent the usual presents interchanged between kings to Benhadad of Damascus, and made alliance against Israel; but Ahab defeated the Syrians at Aphek on the cliffs east of the Sea of Galilee, though Ramoth Gilead (now *Reimûn*) in North Gilead

---

[1] See note, p. 162.

was retained by Syria after three years' war. About half a century later another Benhadad was slain by Hazael, who attacked Gilead and marched into Moab. These internal conflicts were only abated when the Assyrians pressed down from the north and forced Jehu to give tribute to Shalmaneser II.

The "black obelisk" of this Assyrian invader records his victories in Syria. At the beginning of his reign, in 858 B.C., he captured Carchemish, and so gained the passage of the Euphrates, after defeating the Hittites at Pethor, west of the river. A league of Syrian kings was formed against him, including Hittite princes and Phœnicians from the western shores; and though he claims a victory over their forces, in which 20,500 men were slain, his advance was stayed by the Syrian allies. In the eleventh year of his reign he penetrated to Hamath, and in 846 B.C. he attacked the land of Yadai in the extreme north of Syria. Four years later he cut down the cedars of Amanus—the northern Lebanon; and in the next year he took from Hazael of Damascus 1121 chariots and 470 horses. He visited Amanus in the two following years, and took four cities from Hazael; but later expeditions were led against tribes in the Taurus, and the revolt of Hamath was not put down till an Assyrian general advanced south in 832 B.C.

A generation elapsed before Rimmon Nirari, grandson of Shalmaneser II., in 803 B.C., again entered Syria, and advanced as far as Tyre and Sidon; and during this interval Jeroboam II. attacked the exhausted Syrians, and conquered Damascus and Hamath for Israel. The inscription of Panammu I., recently found at Samala, shows us that native Syrian princes were still independent of Assyria about the close of the ninth century B.C.; but about 745 B.C. Assur Nirari II. advanced on Aleppo and on Arpad, and the conquest of Syria was only delayed by revolution in Assyria itself.

A new dynasty arose under Tiglath Pileser III., the conqueror of Syria. After two years' siege he took Arpad and advanced on Hamath. In 743 B.C. he was ruler of Carchemish, Samala, Hamath, Gebal, and Tyre; and in 738 B.C. he replaced rebellious Hamathites by colonists from the Tigris. The author of the Book of Kings (2 Kings xiv. 28) agrees that Hamath was allied to Azariah, king of Judah. In 734 B.C. Tiglath Pileser took 700 captives from Samala, with sheep and oxen, to Assyria. The policy of deportation—pursued later against Israel and Judah—seems to have begun during this reign; but as early as the sixteenth century B.C. the Egyptians held as hostages the sons of Hittite and Amorite chiefs. Captivity began before the Exodus, and was the fate of the vanquished in all later ages.

In 732 B.C. Damascus fell, and Samala submitted to Assyrian rule, as we learn from the inscription left by its Syrian prince, Bar Recab, son of Panammu II., son of Bar Sur, who contrasts the prosperity of his kingdom of Yadai with its misery while opposing Assyria, and speaks of the restoration of the captives whom Tiglath Pileser III. states that he had taken thence. This condition of semi-independence in Samala did not last long, for in 680 B.C. we find an Assyrian ruler established in the city. The conquests of Tiglath Pileser were pushed to Hamath and Gebal, and among his tributaries we read of Rezin in Damascus, Hiram of Tyre, Pekah of Samaria, and Ahaz of Judah. He overran Bashan, Ammon, Moab, and Edom, and subdued Ascalon and Gaza in Philistia. The tribute of Ahaz was sent to Damascus when it was taken in 732 B.C. The Bible tells us also (2 Kings xvi. 7) that Ahaz allied himself with Tiglath Pileser, in consequence of Rezin's raid on the Jews in Edom, and that he sent the treasures of the Jerusalem temple as a present to the invader, going himself to Damascus to meet him. Both date and names and historic statements are thus in accord as regards these events independently recorded by Hebrew and Assyrian chronicles. Ten years later, in 722 B.C., Hamath revolted against Sargon, but the conquest of Syria was practically made by Tiglath Pileser III.

Menahem of Israel had also presented tribute to this conqueror; but the fall of Samaria followed shortly, when Sargon took it in 722 B.C. The attack on Jerusalem began in 702 B.C.; but here the Assyrians were checked for a time, and Judah was saved from ruin for a century by Hezekiah's courage.

Sennacherib's court historian tells us that his master defeated Tirhakah of Egypt near Joppa, and advanced on Ekron. He established a king of the Philistines independent of Hezekiah, from whom he claims to have received thirty talents of gold and eight hundred talents of silver, an ivory throne, with precious woods, gems, eunuchs, horses, mules, asses, camels, oxen, and sheep. Forty-six fortresses of Hezekiah's kingdom were besieged with engines of war; but the capture of Jerusalem is not recorded, and the scribe passes on to relate the victories of the next twenty years in the farther east. He tells us nothing of the reasons for the Assyrian retreat, though the murder of Sennacherib, and accession of his son, Esarhaddon, in 681 B.C., are monumentally confirmed. In the Bible account, and in Herodotus, a disaster is noticed which led to the failure of the attack on Egypt. An inscription of Tirhakah, while saying nothing of the first defeat near Joppa, informs us that the Egyptians pursued the invaders to Syria, and drove them over the Euphrates. It was to Egypt in Isaiah's time that the Hebrews looked for help. The history is only made complete by comparison of Hebrew, Assyrian, and Egyptian records. The Bible tells us nothing of the later years of Sennacherib, but only that "he departed, and went and returned, and dwelt at Nineveh" (2 Kings xix. 36). The Book of Kings (xx. 12) speaks, however, of a later alliance between Hezekiah and Babylon against the common enemy. Merodach Baladan, the king there mentioned, had suffered from Sennacherib in 703 B.C., when his palace was spoiled, and he again revolted in 696 B.C. To conclude that the Hebrew historian believed that Sennacherib died immediately after returning to Nineveh is to ignore his exact words, and to make a needless difficulty in the history of Hezekiah.

In 670 B.C. Esarhaddon took Memphis, after which he reckons among his tributaries the kings of Tyre and Gebal, Arvad, Cyprus, and Palestine. He rebuilt Babylon, and he speaks of Manasseh as his tributary. It is therefore by no means impossible that this king was carried captive by Assyrians to Babylon itself. There is a gap in the monumental comparative history at this point, due to the weakness of Assyria after the prosperous reign of Assur-bani-pal. In 606 B.C. Nineveh fell to the Medes and Babylonians, and the independence of Josiah coincides with this period. After the great battle at Carchemish, between Necho of Egypt and Nebuchadnezzar, in 609 B.C., the tide of Babylonian conquest rolled southwards over Palestine. In 586 B.C. Jerusalem was taken by Nebuchadnezzar (or, as he is more correctly called, Nebuchadrezzar), and fifty years of exile for Judah followed, until the power of the Persians was established by Cyrus, after his conquest of Nabonidus of Babylon. The priests and princes of Judah were carried to Babylon, as Israel had been carried a century earlier to Nineveh, and only the "poor of the land" were left as "vine-dressers and husbandmen" under a Babylonian governor. The story of the Book of Kings, drawn from the archives of the two kingdoms, is thus confirmed by independent records. Only the tradition of the lives of Elijah and Elisha, penned three centuries after their death, remains unnoticed in the Assyrian chronicles, as seemingly in those which related the acts of kings of Israel and of Judah. It used to be argued that the power and civil-

The Siloam Inscription (tracing from a squeeze, taken 15th July, 1881, by Lieuts. Conder and Mantell, R.E.).

isation of the Hebrews in Hezekiah's age were over-represented by the Hebrew writers. We have now, on the contrary, Sennacherib's own account of Hezekiah's wealth: we have an extant inscription at Siloam which shows us the language and written character of Judah in his time: we have the actual remains of the great tunnel from the Upper Gihon, which led "by an underground channel" "westwards to the city of David," just as described in Chronicles. The suspicions of those who denied the early civilisation of the Hebrews, and the truth of their history, are not confirmed, but, on the contrary, confuted, by what is known up to to-day from monuments of Egyptians, Moabites, Syrians, and Assyrians, from one Hebrew text at Jerusalem itself, and from the actual remains of the aqueduct prepared before the Assyrian armies had advanced on Judah.

NOTES TO CHAPTER IX.

The Siloam Inscription.—The translation of this text, from the squeeze made by the present author in 1881, is as follows :—

1. The cutting. Now this is the method of the cutting: while the workers raised
2. the axe each to his fellow, and three cubits were left, each heard the voice of the other calling
3. to his fellow, for there was an excess of rock to the right and . . .
4. the cutting, the workers hewed each to meet his fellow axe to axe, and there flowed
5. the waters from the spring to the pool a thousand two hundred cubits, and . . .
6. cubit was the height of the rock [over the heads of the workers?]

The point of junction was determined by the Survey party near the middle of the tunnel, and the length as chained proved to be 1200 cubits of about 16 inches, which length of cubit also agrees with the measurements of the Galilean synagogues and of the Temple ramparts, as well as with the statements of the Jewish scholar Maimonides concerning the cubit. See Conder's 'Handbook to the Bible,' and 'Memoirs of the Survey of Western Palestine'—Jerusalem volume, under Birket Silwan. The "conduit" is mentioned in 2 Kings xx. 20, and more fully in 2 Chron. xxxii. 30. The object appears to have been to collect the waters of Gihon (now 'Ain Umm ed Deraj), flowing originally down the Kidron valley, and to bring them " by an underground channel westwards to the city of David," where, in the Pool of Siloam, they were within bow-shot of the wall above. A staircase in the rock led down, from within the wall, to the back of the rock-cut pool of Gihon.

Chronology of the Book of Kings.—The difficulty in treating Old Testament chronology by itself lies in the variations between the versions. Thus while the Hebrew text gives a total of 1946 years, from Adam to Terah, the Samaritan makes this total 2247 years, and the Greek Septuagint 3412 years. In the Book of Kings not only are there differences between the versions, but the different totals of the kings of Israel and Judah are only explicable by supposing an interregnum. Joram of Israel and Ahaziah of Judah died at the same time (2 Kings ix. 22-27), and the fall of Samaria is said to have occurred in the sixth year of Hezekiah of Judah —the ninth of Hoshea of Israel; but the details of the intervening kings of Israel amount to 143 years for ten kings, whereas the seven kings of Judah (including six years for Hezekiah) are reckoned as amounting to 165 years during the same interval. Only one invasion of Palestine is monumentally recorded of Sennacherib, in 702 B.C. That mentioned in the Bible is said to have occurred in the fourteenth year of Hezekiah (2 Kings xviii. 13), or eight years after the fall of Samaria in 722 B.C. There is thus a discrepancy of twelve or thirteen years, and as Hezekiah reigned for twenty-nine years it is probable that the numbers have been corrupted, and that the invasion occurred in his twenty-sixth year. Instances of the differences between the versions include the reading eighteenth for second year of Jehoram (2 Kings i. 17) in the Greek, thirty-ninth for thirty-seventh year (2 Kings xiii. 10) for Joash, according to the Greek, with other variations in the chronology of Jeremiah. As already noticed, the numeral signs used on monuments, and probably used in the records consulted by the author of Kings, are very liable to corruption. The total of the kings of Judah from the fall of Samaria to the close of the reign of Zedekiah (136 years) appears to be correctly preserved within one or two years.

Under these circumstances the monumental dates are of high value, since we are able to consult originals which have not suffered at the hands of later copyists. The eponym lists, which give the names of Assyrian officials for consecutive years in the ninth, eighth, and seventh centuries B.C., were discovered by Layard and other excavators at Nineveh, and studied by Sir H. Rawlinson ('Athenæum,' 1862, &c.): four copies exist which supplement each other's deficiencies, and three other brief summaries of historic events. In one case an eclipse of the sun, occurring in the month Sivan, fixes the eponym year of Purilsagali in 763 B.C. Hence the contemporary reigns of Jehu, Menahem, Pekah, and Hoshea of Israel, and of Azariah, Ahaz, and Hezekiah of Judah, are checked by the reigns of Shalmaneser II., Tiglath Pileser III., Sargon (who refers to the capture of Samaria), and Sennacherib. The reference on the Moabite Stone to the days of Omri and half the reign of Ahab, as amounting to "forty years," is less important. The Bible gives 33 years for the total of the two reigns, but the Moabite statement is probably only a rough estimate. When we remember that our earliest manuscripts of the Old Testament only take us back to about the tenth century A.D., or 1600 years later than the time when the Book of Kings was written, we can only wonder that the numerical discrepancies are so slight, and must recognise the genuine character of the Hebrew records, as compared with the ancient tablets of the century preceding the captivity of Judah.

The chronology of the kings, checked by monumental dates, appears most perfect in the list of Judah, as below :—

FIRST PERIOD.

	Reigns years.		Reigns years.	
Rehoboam	18	Jeroboam	22	
Abijam	3	Nadab	2	
Asa	41	Baashah	13	from 3rd Asa
Jehosaphat	25	Elah	1	„ 16th „
Joram	8	Zimri	11	„ 17th „
Ahaziah	1	Omri	11	„ 28th „
		Ahab	22	
		Ahaziah	2	
		Joram	12	
Total	96	Total	96	

CHRONOLOGY OF THE BOOK OF KINGS. 161

SECOND PERIOD.

	Reigns years.		Reigns years.
Athaliah	6	Jehu	34
Joash	40	Jehoahaz	12 (O.T. 17)
Amaziah	29	Joash	17 from 38th Joash
Azariah	52	Jeroboam II.	52 " 15th Amaziah
Jotham	6 (O.T. 16)	Zechariah	1 " 38th Azariah
Ahaz	13 (O.T. 16)	Shallum	0
6th Hezekiah	6	Menahem	20 " 39th "
		Pekahiah	2
		Pekah	2 Monuments
		Hoshea	12 "
Total	152	Total	152

The resulting dates agree with all monumental notices :—

B.C.
- 970. Rehoboam accedes in Judah, Jeroboam in Israel.
- 966. Shishak accedes in Egypt.
- 965. Shishak attacks Palestine.
- 952. Abijam accedes in Judah.
- 949. Asa accedes in Judah.
- 948. Nadab accedes in Israel.
- 946. Baasha accedes in Israel, 3d Asa.
- 933. Elah accedes in Israel, 16th (for 26th) Asa.
- 932. Zimri accedes in Israel, 17th (for 27th) Asa.
- 921. Omri accedes in Israel, 28th (for 38th) Asa.
- 910. Ahab accedes in Israel.
- 908. Jehosaphat accedes in Judah.
- 888. Ahaziah accedes in Israel.
- 886. Joram accedes in Israel.
- 883. Joram accedes in Judah.
- 875. Ahaziah accedes in Judah.
- 874. Jehu's revolt. Athaliah in Jerusalem.
- 867. Joash accedes in Judah.
- 852. Shalmaneser attacks Damascus. Syrian league.
- 840. Jehu's tribute to Shalmaneser. Jehoahaz succeeds him.
- 828. Joash accedes in Israel two years before Amaziah.
- 826. Amaziah accedes in Judah.
- 811. Jeroboam II. accedes in Israel: 15th Amaziah.
- 803. Rimmon Nirari attacks Samaria, Edom, Philistia.
- 796. Azariah accedes in Judah.
- 759. Zechariah accedes in Israel: 38th Azariah.
- 758. Shallum and Menahem accede in Israel: 39th Azariah.
- 743. Tiglath Pileser attacks Arpad.

L

NOTES TO CHAPTER IX.

B.C.
- 742. Azariah's tribute to Tiglath Pileser. Jotham succeeds in Judah.
- 738. Menahem's tribute to Tiglath Pileser. Pekahiah succeeds.
- 736. Ahaz accedes in Judah. Pekah in Israel.
- 734. Tribute of Ahaz to Tiglath Pileser. Attack on Galilee, Samaria, Ammon, Edom, Moab, Gaza. Pekah killed. Hoshea set up by Assyrian king.
- 732. Capture of Rezin in Damascus. Tribute of Ahaz.
- 729. Accession of Hezekiah in Judah.
- 722. Capture of Samaria by Sargon: 6th Hezekiah.
- 711. Ashdod taken by Sargon.
- 705. Accession of Sennacherib.
- 704. First attack on Merodach Baladan in Babylon.
- 702. Sennacherib attacks Philistia and Judah.
- 701. Defeat of Sennacherib by Tirhakah of Egypt.
- 699. Manasseh accedes in Judah. Tributary 671-668 B.C.
- 681. Sennacherib murdered by a son. Esarhaddon accedes.
- 680. Esarhaddon attacks Egypt.
- 668. Assurbanipal accedes in Assyria.
- 664. Assurbanipal takes Thebes (Nahum iii. 8).
- 643. Amon accedes in Judah.
- 641. Josiah accedes in Judah.
- 609. Necho attacks Assyria. Death of Josiah.
- 606. Fall of Nineveh.
- 605. Nebuchadnezzar accedes in Babylon.
- 598. Jehoiakin accedes in Judah. First captivity of Judah.
- 597. Zedekiah succeeds in Judah.
- 586. Destruction of Jerusalem by Nebuchadnezzar.

This chronology differs from that of Professor Kamphausen, who cuts off ten years from the reigns of Amaziah, Azariah, Jotham, and Manasseh, for which changes there is no literary or monumental authority.

The Site of Tarshish.—The old theory that Tarshish was Tartessus in Spain was based on the supposition that tin was only to be found, in ancient days, in the Scilly Islands, and brought by the Phœnicians from the far west to Asia. The Scilly Islands were not unknown to Herodotus in the Persian age, but the Phœnician trade with Spain and Britain was founded by the Carthaginians between 800 and 600 B.C., and the colony at Tartessus cannot be supposed to have existed as

THE SITE OF TARSHISH. 163

early as Solomon's time, since Carthage was not founded till about two centuries later (143 years after the Temple was built, according to Josephus, against Apion, i. 18). Silver, lead, iron, and (by trade) tin could be found in Spain; but they were known from the earliest age in Asia, tin coming either from the Caucasus or perhaps from the Altai Mountains. In Genesis (x. 4) Tarshish is named with Ionia and Cyprus as inhabited by the "fair" race. In 1 Kings x. 22 we read that the Hebrew and Tyrian fleet brought from Tarshish gold, silver, ivory, apes (*kophim*), and peacocks (*tukkeim*). "Ships of Tarshish" are, however, noticed as trading with Ophir (near Sheba in Arabia, Gen. x. 28, 29) in 1 Kings xxii. 48; 2 Chron. xx. 36. The captives of Judah are to return from Tarshish (Isa. lx. 9), which is again named with Lydia, Tubal, and Ionia in Asia Minor (Isa. lxvi. 19). Ezekiel speaks of the Tyrian trade with Tarshish in silver, iron, tin, and lead (xxvii. 12), and also apparently of the other Tarshish near Sheba (xxxviii. 13). The trade in metals with Asia Minor was ancient; for in the Tell Amarna letters ships from Elishah are noticed bringing gold, copper, and silver (Nos. 5, 6, 7, British Museum collection; 12, 15, Berlin collection), as well as bronze, which supposes the existence of tin (No. 6, British Museum), and apparently ivory (No. 14, Berlin), which also came from Babylon (No. 4, British Museum). Hence the trade products of Tarshish could all be obtained in Solomon's time from Tarsus on the Asia Minor coast, which appears to have been the Mediterranean Tarshish (Jonah i. 3, iv. 2). It is not probable that ivory, apes, and peacocks would have borne Indian names at Tartessus in Spain, and they must have come by the overland route from the east to Tarsus, unless the southern Tarshish in Arabia is intended, when they may have come from Somaliland—a view favoured by the Egyptian names (*ɩb*) for elephant and (*kafi*) for ape. Tarsus on the Cydnus was still approachable by galleys in Cleopatra's time.

CHAPTER X.

THE PROPHETS.

The great historic value of the prophetic books lies, as already shown, in their references to past events in Hebrew history, and to the rites, the customs, and the Law of Israel. The high religious tone of Isaiah and his brethren contrasts with the idolatry of the nation at large, while the decay of the Hebrew race is witnessed by the denunciation of tyranny, luxury, and drunkenness among their rich men and princes. We learn also more of Hebrew beliefs regarding God and the future from the Prophets than we do from the Law, concerned rather with worldly affairs. The hope that a future ideal king would arise from David's house is often expressed; but the prediction of a Messiah, such as all the world expected in the century before Christ, does not find distinct expression in the Prophets before the Exile.

It is often said that the early Hebrews had no belief in any future life. That there is no allusion to a kingdom of heaven on earth, and to a thousand years in which the risen righteous should live under the Messiah in the Holy Land—as the Pharisees taught later—is no doubt true; but the picture which Isaiah draws (xiv.) of a tyrant entering Sheol, and sadly received by royal ghosts,[1] shows us that, like the Akkadians, the Egyptians, the Assyrians, and Phœnicians, the Hebrews believed in a dim under-world, where shades of the departed lived in peace or in sorrow, according to the judgment passed upon their earthly life by the great Judge of the dead. There is no distinction between this common Asiatic belief and that of the Greeks in Homer. The under-world of Sheol is also mentioned in the Pentateuch itself, and the judgment-day by Joel (Num. xvi. 30; Joel iii.)

Up to the fortieth chapter the Book of Isaiah is full of reference to the politics of his age, and includes the historic chapters relating Hezekiah's deliverance from Sennacherib. Two chapters have been suspected by critics (xiii. and xxi. 1-10) because of references to Babylon, to the Medes, and to Elam. But when we consider that the Assyrians were already in conflict with the Medes in 850 B.C., that their quarrel with Elam was ancient (for Elam was attacked by Rimmon Nirari in the ninth century B.C.), and that Merodach Baladan was attacked in Babylon by the Assyrians in 710, 703, and 696 B.C., we gather that a reference to the destruction of Babylon is natural in Isaiah's time. Hezekiah allied himself to Merodach Baladan in the latter year, 696 B.C., but on this alliance Isaiah looked with disfavour. It is not, therefore, unnatural that he should rejoice in the destruction of the city in 703 B.C., before the Assyrians

[1] See note p. 171.

had become the open enemies of Judah. Another chapter (xxvii.) has been doubted mainly because it speaks of the outcasts of Israel in Egypt and Assyria; but Israel was already captive in Nineveh in 722 B.C., and other Hebrews may have been removed by Tirhakah to Egypt after his defeat of Sennacherib. The first allusion to a doctrine of immortality is found in an early chapter of Isaiah (xxvi. 19), "Awake and sing, ye that dwell in the dust: . . . for earth shall bring to life the shades."

But, as is well known, the last twenty-six chapters of our Book of Isaiah have long been attributed by scholars to a later age, and to an unknown prophet of the time of Cyrus. The reasons are simple, and require no great learning to understand. Cyrus is mentioned not as a future but as a present ruler (xlv. 1), and Babylon as conquered (xlvi., xlvii.) The sons of Judah are about to leave the land of exile (xlviii. 20), to become priests of Jehovah among the strangers who had been brought into Palestine by the Babylonians (lxi. 6). The Assyrian is mentioned as an oppressor in the past (lii. 4), and though the exhortation is addressed to a despairing people (xl. 27), it is not to the same faint-hearted nation in Jerusalem itself whom Isaiah addressed, but to a nation exhorted to return thither. The prophet seems to refer (xlii. 9) to the fulfilment of Isaiah's former prophecies of general destruction to the ancient world, and of captivity for Judah in Babylon,—"Behold, the former things are come to pass, and new things do I declare." He laments the unbelief of the nation (liii. 1), and perhaps alludes to

Isaiah himself as despised and rejected. The time of Cyrus is one which answers well to the requirements of these chapters, and they are hard to reconcile with an earlier age.

Among the minor prophets Amos, who wrote about 746 B.C., is probably the oldest. His prophecies concern the history of his age, and contain many allusions to Hebrew customs, to the "songs of the Temple" (viii. 3), to the music of David (vi. 5), to the idol shrines at Bethel and Gilgal. Hosea, his contemporary, preserves yet more allusions to the early history of the Hebrews, and speaks of the written Law. The latest date given for his writings is 722 B.C. Micah, about this same date, resembles both the preceding. Zephaniah follows a century later, just before Josiah's reformation in 621 B.C.; and Nahum, who records the ruin of Nineveh and the earlier destruction of Thebes in Egypt, appears to have written after 607 B.C. Habakkuk was his contemporary. Haggai and Zechariah prophesied after the return from exile, about 520 B.C.; and Malachi closes the list of minor prophets in 430 B.C. Three books remain, however, less clearly dated —namely, Joel, who is sometimes thought to have lived in the ninth century B.C., and who mentions the Ionians with the Egyptians and Edomites—an uncertain mark of date; Obadiah, who speaks of the pride of Edom, which may refer to several periods of history; and, finally, the story of Jonah—undated save by its language, which seems possibly to be late. The expression "God of heaven" (Jonah i. 9) is one commonly used after the

Captivity; and the date at which Jonah himself lived (2 Kings xiv. 25), in the ninth century B.C., does not of necessity date the book which contains his story. It may have been written four hundred years later.

In thus considering the twelve minor prophets, we have passed beyond the age of Jeremiah. His book is one of the few which have not been questioned by critics, and it contains a storehouse of illustrations for Hebrew history about the close of the seventh century and opening of the sixth century B.C. It is remarkable that the Greek text presents more differences from the Hebrew than in any other book except Samuel; and about an eighth part of the Hebrew is missing in the Septuagint translation, while the order of chapters is different. It is probable that it was translated much later than the Pentateuch, and an imperfect copy seems to have been used for the Greek. The name of Nebuchadrezzar is correctly given in this book (li. 34), which closes with a historical chapter, and tells us something also of events after the Babylonian destruction of Jerusalem. Acquaintance with the Law influences Jeremiah's tone and language, and his spirit is less sacerdotal than that of Ezekiel his successor, who was carried to Babylon in 597 B.C., and prophesied as late as 570 B.C. in the land of exile. The language of Ezekiel is thought to bear some traces of Aramean influence, but differs from that of the age of Ezra; and it was not until more than a century after Nebuchadnezzar's time that the new Hebrew began to be distinguishable from the classic tongue of Isaiah's age. To Ezekiel we owe the remarkable account of Tyrian trade about 600 B.C. (xxvii.), when Armenia, Syria, and Arabia, Asia Minor and Egypt, sent their wares to the Phœnician capital. His description of the Temple served in part as a model in the later time of Herod; but the new division of Palestine among the tribes, and the new arrangement of land for the Levites, were ideal, and never carried out. They are chiefly interesting in connection with the Bible account, as showing that the allotment of Joshua is ancient and actual, while that of Ezekiel is future, and never put into real operation.

This short sketch of the writings of the Prophets serves to control the references already made to their evidence. They allude generally to the events of their own times, or of the immediate future; but they look forward also to the "branch" to spring from David's house, and to rule a united Israel. The Book of Daniel has not been forgotten in this enumeration, for it has never formed part of the Hebrew canon of the Prophets. The distinction of a second writer, following Isaiah in the times of Cyrus, is perhaps one of the soundest—but by no means of the most recent—results of literary study of the Bible itself. Similar results must be mentioned later, which stand on a very different basis from that of the critical theories propounded lately as to the Law and early Hebrew records.

NOTE TO CHAPTER X.

The Hebrew Belief in the Future.—Nothing is more unfounded than the statement that the Hebrews had no belief in existence after death. In Isaiah (xiv.) the king of Babylon is represented as entering Sheol (verse 9), where he is met by the dead, and the *rephaim* or "ghosts" of other kings, who say, "Art thou become weak as we?" The *rephaim* or ghosts are also mentioned in the inscription of Eshmunazar of Sidon (third century B.C.) There are allusions to Sheol in the Pentateuch itself (Num. xvi. 30, 33; Deut. xxxii. 22); and in Samuel the prophet is represented as dwelling in Sheol (1 Sam. xxviii. 13, 19). The common Semitic belief is indicated by Assyrian tablets, and by designs on seals. The supreme judge of the dead was believed to dwell under the sea, and the ghosts were brought before him for judgment. Those who had been righteous enjoyed peace in Hades, under a "silver sky," while the wicked were tormented. As among the Greeks, this condition appears to have been regarded as final and unending. The Egyptians, on the other hand, believed in a final return to the body, which they embalmed—a practice which seems to have been uncommon among Semitic peoples.

CHAPTER XI.

HEBREW POETRY.

WE have found no reason to suppose that the Hebrews were inferior to their neighbours in literary power. The religious tone of Isaiah surpasses anything known in monumental texts, and the very early date at which eloquent poetry is found, both in Egypt and in Mesopotamia, witnesses the early date at which it also existed among Hebrews. The psalm of Thothmes III., and the poem of Pentaur on the victory of Rameses II. at Kadesh, are good Egyptian examples,[1] dating earlier than David's time; but yet more ancient passages in Akkadian texts may be quoted, as bearing strong resemblance in thought and style to Hebrew poetry.

The most ancient example — older than the days of Abraham — is found in the curse, written in Akkadian, on Gudea's statue at Zirghul — written "for him who knows not, in future days after many generations." The man who should remove the statue or injure the inscription is thus denounced:—

"May the mighty in his time destroy, may the power of the multitude rise as a storm. May the man who does this to me sit

---

[1] Brugsch, Hist. Egypt, vol. i. p. 370; vol. ii. p. 44.

in the dust as a slave. May his name of renown become a name of weakness. May his name be smitten by the gods. May the seed of his posterity perish, his name becoming a perished name. The gods destroying his people before his eyes, may heaven's wind destroy, may the waters destroy his land. The people that is a foe of that man's land being enemies, may his city perish from the light of heaven. May the gods so teach the people, their hand making an end."

The vigour and eloquence of this language is very remarkable at so early a period. But other Akkadian songs and psalms were copied from the "ancient original," and translated into Assyrian for Assurbanipal, in the seventh century B.C., and to these translations our knowledge of Akkadian is due.[1] The date of the originals, which were already ancient, is not known; but it is thought that Akkadian began to become a dead language as early as 1500 B.C., and their antiquity must at least be equal to that of any Hebrew poetry.

One of these poems is a short war-song of early character :—

"Leading the herd,
You trod the young corn.
I go knee-deep,
I stay not my foot.
Not first in fault
My host obeys me.

You come and waste
The foeman's field.
He comes and wastes
Thy field, O foe.

The corn grows high,
What care we.
The corn is ripe,
What care we.

The lot of death
Be thine to taste.
The lot of life
May I enjoy."

Such a war-song we may well imagine sung by invaders even in Abraham's days.

[1] See note, p. 192.

Another early poem recently found is the Akkadian account of Creation:—

"The bright abode of gods on high was not created. No plant had grown, no tree had been created. No brick was laid, no beam was hewn, no house was built, no town was founded." "He made mankind." "He made the beasts of the field, and living things in the desert. He made the Tigris and Euphrates, and set them in their place, and called them by name. He made the herb, the reed, and the forest. He made the grass of the plain, the field, the marsh and the wood alike, oxen and their young, the cow and her calf, the sheep in field, meadow, and forest, the goat and the stag."[1]

The general resemblance of this fragment to the first chapter of Genesis is notable, but over-elaboration weakens its power as compared with the Hebrew. Creation is, even in the Akkadian account, attributed to a single Creator. Such poems addressed to a single god are, however, in some cases only in praise of one among many, as in another instance when Merodach the Sun-god is thus hymned:—

"Who may escape thy terrors? . . . Thy word is a great decree which rules the heaven and the earth. It bade the sea, and she stayed her waves. It bade the storm, and it was still. It bade the flood of the Euphrates — the word of Merodach troubled its waves. Thou art great among gods, O Merodach, who is like thee?"

The fate of the wicked is the subject of another of these Akkadian poems translated into Assyrian:—

"With aching head he wanders, as in a desert when the storm blows, and the lightning flashes and falls from on high. He who

---

[1] Translated by Mr T. G. Pinches, 'Journal of the Royal Asiatic Society,' 1893.

fears not his god is broken as a reed, and his sore runs as a stream. He who has not Ashtoreth for his guide, his flesh is wasted: he fades as a star from heaven: he goes to the night like water. He is hated by all who pass by, and is as though the daylight burned him. That man is bowed as if by pangs of the heart, he is distracted as one whose heart pants. He burns as one on fire, as the wild ass raging when the storm is in its eyes. For his life is devoured and he hastens to death, distraught as when the storm is mighty. None knows whither he goes. None knows the last fate that overtakes him."

There is a general resemblance between this ancient poem and passages in Job; but other Akkadian psalms are yet closer to the Hebrew in thought and imagery :—

"How long, O God, who knowest the unknown, shall Thy heart be wroth? How long, O mother Ashtoreth, who knowest the unknown, shall thy heart be wroth? She has made a narrow way for men, and none knows it; of all men who are named none knows it. O Lord, Thou wilt not reject Thy servant. O grant me this, to take his hand in the waters of the stream. Turn away my sins that I have wrought for Thy mercies' sake. Let the wind carry away the sin that I have wrought. The greatness of my shame covers me as a garment. O my God, forgive the sins that I have wrought till seven times seven. O pardon my neglect, O defend Thy servant. Let Thy heart turn to this place as a mother to her child. O return as father and as mother to this place."

This prayer, entitled "The lamentations of an humble heart," was no doubt originally carved on some Akkadian statue or stored in a temple. Another fragment refers to sickness :—

"I sit and mourn: the heart faints by the curse of sickness. I mourn as a dove night and day. The groans of the sick are made to his God as a child for pity. His face is bowed with lamentation to his God."

Yet another tablet contains prayers to Ashtoreth in both languages:—

"The face of all creation is bowed." "O give rest to thy servant, I said, O merciful one, thou receivest him who has erred. The man thou favourest that man shall live. O power in all things, Lady pitying man, receiver of lamentations, whom it is good to seek: Mother Goddess, thou takest the hand of him who thus earnestly calls on thee. There is none greater than the gracious Goddess. O favour thou me fully, hear my cry, decree my pardon, and let thy wrath be appeased. How long, O Lady, shall thy face be dark? I mourn as a dove, I groan groans, O let me rest in peace."

"How long, O Lady, shall the foe lay waste?" "In thy great city of Erech there is fasting. In the temple of star-gazing—the temple of thy oracle—the blood flows like water. I have made the fires hot throughout the land." "O my Lady, I have restrained the slanderer, my hand has broken the wicked man as a reed. I wrest not the law, I am not proud. Yet I waste away like water day and night. I am thy servant, I testify to thee. Let thy servant be exalted, let thy people increase."

This last passage is interesting as showing that the Akkadian psalms belonged to Erech, the great temple city in Southern Chaldea, which was the capital of the early Akkadian princes. The antiquity of the originals copied —before the captivity of Judah—for Assurbanipal may thus be carried back possibly to 2000 B.C. The language often recalls that of Hebrew psalms of later date, but the double appeals to god and goddess are distinctive of an earlier heathen creed.

By the light of such comparison we may read the Book of Job, the Psalms, the Song of Solomon, the Proverbs, and the Preacher, without supposing that all such works among the Hebrews must have been written in a later

M

age, when the spirit of the nation had decayed, and when the language of Isaiah's time was corrupted.

The Book of Job is remarkable, it is true, for many words comparable with Aramaic and Arabic, but its language also compares with that of Amos and Isaiah. The scene is laid in the country round Petra, and the notices of the ostrich and the wild ass, of mines and gems, of frost and heat, all point to the southern deserts; while the horse, the city with its gates, the astronomical knowledge of the rising of stars in their seasons, forbid us to suppose an author entirely unacquainted with settled life. The land of Uz, though wrongly placed by Christian tradition in Bashan, is very clearly indicated in the Bible to have lain in Edom, where Arab tribes of Nabatheans were settled as early as the eighth century B.C., according to monumental records. The language of Job—like that of the Moabite Stone—was apparently affected by local dialects. The author speaks in no part of Israel or of the Law, and though probably a Hebrew, may have lived among the Nabathean tribes, and have spoken an Edomite dialect of the Hebrew language. We have already seen that Hebrew tribes invaded Edom in the times of David and of Hezekiah, and were there found much later (1 Chron. iv. 31).

There is little to indicate the date of this magnificent poem. The name of Satan, found in its first chapter, only occurs in other cases in books written in Ezra's age or later, but the language is not that of Ezra's time. The name of Job, like that of Daniel, was known to Ezekiel

(xiv. 11, 20 xxviii. 3); but this does not prove the existence of the present Book of Job. The subject of the poem is the reason for evil in the world, explained as being hidden from man, but known to God. The prosperity of the wicked and the misfortunes of the good are shown to be due to hidden purpose. The justice of God is slow but sure; and if not in this world, yet in the future the wicked will give account for their evil deeds. To the very end the cause of Job's downfall—intended by God as a reproof to the sneering Satan—is never revealed to Job. His friends suspect some sin committed by their fallen friend, and goad him to madness by their hints that punishment must have a reason. He answers always that he knows his own innocence, and would plead it with God were he able. Elihu alone strikes a truer note, though equally ignorant of the great cause. He exhorts Job to humble himself before God, and foresees that his misery is but a passing cloud. It is strange that some authors should regard the speeches of Elihu as later additions, interrupting the poem, which without them would be imperfect. They argue that Elihu does not appear earlier in the book, and is unnoticed in the last chapter. The book itself explains most clearly why he is not noticed at first (Job xxxii. 2-6), while in the end he is not mentioned because he was not condemned, and needed no intercession with God. Elihu is a Hebrew name (1 Sam. i. 1), but his tribe was Edomite: his speech leads up to the final crisis of the poem, as he watches the great thunderstorm approaching (xxxvi. 26-33, xxxvii. 1-22), and likens its passing, when "fair weather comes from the dark," to Job's passing troubles. The voice of Jehovah from the whirlwind is thus naturally the sequel (xxxviii. 1). If Elihu's speeches are cut out no answer is given by man to Job's complaint, and no teaching completes the book; for the cause of evil is not explained in the magnificent chapters which describe creation by the mouth of God. If Jehovah answered Job at once there is a manifest break in the notice of the whirlwind, which is described by Elihu at the close of his speech.

The antiquity and unity of the Book of Job are on these grounds evident, although the date cannot be established very closely. The author was a servant of Jehovah, but the name is not supposed to have been known to the Edomites, and Job—until Jehovah reveals Himself to him—seems rather to have been a pious foreigner than a disciple of Moses. He eschewed idolatry, and offered sacrifices to God (i. 5, xxxi. 26), and acted justly to all: but the Syrians also sacrificed in 800 B.C., as the Samala inscription tells us; and ethical precepts go back to a very early age in Egypt, and in Akkadian tablets, which command the veneration of parents and justice to the poor. "I have heard of Thee by the hearing of the ear; but now mine eye seeth Thee" (xlii. 5), are the words of Job, as though a stranger to the name of Jehovah before that time, hearing His name as that of a distant God among the Israelites. The worship of Jehovah among other nations besides the Hebrews is not only clear from monuments, but is noticed in the prophets from the eighth century B.C. downwards.[1] The answer of the philosopher in Job, to the ever-recurring question of the origin of evil, is that which was commonly given by many nations from the earliest historic ages — the hidden purpose of God. Even the visible creation, he says, is beyond our understanding, how much more the purpose of the Creator who guides it, and bends the good and the wicked alike to that purpose. Nor can we say that modern philosophies give us more light on such a question, or tell us more certainly of the future, or of the mysteries whereby we are surrounded. The Hebrew answer remains still true—"Such knowledge is too wonderful for me."

The Book of Psalms is commonly ascribed to David, although the titles of the Psalms—which are as old at least as the time of the Greek translators—ascribe several to Asaph, Korah, and others, and to Moses and Solomon. No careful reader is likely to hold that the sad psalm of captivity "by the waters of Babylon" (cxxxvii.) can have been written in David's time. The Hebrew text divides the Psalter into five books, of which the first three contains 64 psalms attributed to David, 12 to Korah, 12 to Asaph, and 1 to Ethan. If all David's psalms originally stood together (i.-xli., li.-lxxii.), the other psalms might be later; but as they are now arranged, the original collection seems to close with the words (Ps. lxxii. 20), "The prayers of David the son of Jesse are ended." In this collection two of the psalms which are alphabetic were

[1] See Isa. xxxvi. 7-10, lxv. 1; Mal. i. 11.

once clearly one (xlii.-xliii.), as in some manuscripts, and this gives us a total of 88 ancient psalms, including six which are alphabetic (Ps. ix., xxv., xxxiv., xxxvii., xlii., xliii.) Alphabetic psalms suppose the existence of an alphabet; but as this was probably in use in David's time, this indication is unimportant. Nor is the use of the words Elohim and Jehovah of great value, if graphic rather than literary reasons be assigned for the difference. In the Psalter are found repetitions (Ps. xl. 13-17 and lxx.; and Ps. cviii. compared with lvii. 5-11, lx. 5-12), in some cases showing the name Jehovah instead of Elohim. If the original psalm was written on a tablet, and the name of the Deity marked by an emblem (as explained already), these differences in transcription would easily be understood. This peculiarity in the Psalter serves, therefore, to confirm that view of Hebrew writing.

As regards the date of the Asaph psalms, one of them (lxxvi.) is ascribed in the Greek version to Assyrian times; but even this does not indicate date, since Assyria and Israel may have been in conflict at least in Solomon's time. It is otherwise with another Asaph psalm (lxxix.) which speaks of the destruction of Jerusalem. It may refer to the attack by Shishak after Solomon's death, but cannot allude to Sennacherib, who never "laid Jerusalem on heaps" (verse 1): the language alone is sufficient to confute the theory that it was written in the Greek age. In yet another Asaph psalm (lxxxiii.) Assur is noticed (verse 8), and it is possible that the psalms not attributed to David are the latest.

A second division (Ps. xc. to end) begins at the end of the present third book, and the language of these psalms is generally later than that of those in the first three books. The name of Jehovah is almost exclusively used; and though some which bear David's name may be recensions of older hymns, they cannot as they now stand belong to David's time. The "songs of degrees" were written for the Temple: the alphabetic psalms (cxi., cxix., cxlv.) are much longer than before: one psalm at least is as late as the Captivity (cxxxviii.); and in another case the Greek bears a title, "When the Temple was built after the Captivity" (xcvi.). To attribute any of these psalms to the later time of the Maccabees (the Greek age) is linguistically impossible, but it is clear that the Psalter was gradually formed between the time of David and of Ezra. One of the earlier psalms (xviii.) is directly attributed by the Hebrew historian (2 Sam. xxii.) to David himself.

Turning to the Song of Songs, we find still more interesting indications of literary variety. The Song of Solomon was only added to the canon by the later Jews, because a mystical meaning was explained to underlie its passionate language. There can be little doubt that the wording is often highly symbolic, and not to be taken in its literal sense as dealing with shepherds or gardeners. The bride is herself compared to a garden and a spring; and the style is not very different from that of later Arab love-songs. Two fragments of Egyptian poems, closely resembling the Song of Songs in style, are known to have been written before Solomon's age. The language of the Song itself is highly peculiar, and though it shows no sign of being late, it is tinged with Aramaic expressions, showing a dialect somewhat different from classical Hebrew.

The critical views as to the explanation of the Song of Songs are hardly satisfactory. It is necessary to remember that the seclusion of women, among the upper classes, is of great antiquity in the East. It is mentioned in patriarchal times in the Bible. It is also necessary to remember that dramatic performances are unknown to have ever occurred among Semitic peoples before the Greek and Roman ages. They are still regarded with disfavour in the East. Again, we must not forget that women were accustomed to share their husband's love with others. No Hebrew woman would have ever demanded that she alone should be her husband's wife.

All these facts are disregarded by critical writers, who advance various explanations of the Song of Songs. In one the engaged couple are supposed to take a walk in the fields, like European lovers of to-day. In another the Shulamite is supposed to escape from Solomon's harem, and to join a rustic lover. The fate of Uriah seems to be forgotten, and the idyl, though possible enough in Schiller's time, does not represent realities of Eastern life. Both these critics agree in supposing a kind of drama, with chorus, dances, and change of scene, of which we have no indications in Semitic antiquity.

THE BRIDEGROOM AND BRIDE.   185

To the student of Arab life the Song of Songs reads very differently from either of these explanations. Its passionate love-language resembles that of Arab songs sung before Muhammad's time; its tone suggests a royal bridal ode, composed perhaps in the distant province whence the Shulamite was brought. Bride and bridegroom answer one another, but such language is hardly to be attributed to an affianced maiden in Hebrew times.

We may, then, attempt briefly to show the indications which the poem includes, and thence draw conclusions as to its origin and meaning. The translation often obscures the latter, and the assumption that the scene is laid in Jerusalem limits the explanation of its origin.

The Song, which stands first among the Hebrew *Megilloth* or "rolls," and which was read in later times during the glad spring feast of Passover, is called distinctly "a song of songs to Solomon." The bride speaks to her lord and says, "If the king brought me to his chambers we would rejoice and be glad." She invokes the daughters of Jerusalem not to scorn her as darker than the Hebrew women of the city, because of her life in the open country. She speaks (after the custom of oriental poetry) symbolically of following a shepherd's journey with his flocks, and is answered in the same strain by the bridegroom. Her humility is expressed in the single verse, "I am but a wild flower of the plains, and a lily of the valleys," with the answer, "As a lily among thorns, is my love among girls." She calls her bridegroom to hasten as a deer, and proclaims her love; but charges the daughters of distant Jerusalem not "to awake love till it please"— a refrain repeated by her at times. She relates the bridegroom's invitation to leave her home, in spring-time, for better lands where the flowers bloom, the dove calls in the woods, and the fig-tree buds, contrasted with the barren mountains and deep valleys of her own country. She speaks of her dream, during the bridegroom's absence, in which he seemed once more to reach her home; and she repeats the refrain—let him not come till he please. She pictures his advance in royal state from the wilderness, crowned with a marriage crown. The bridegroom answers with imagery borrowed from the flocks of Gilead, and David's tower of shields. He calls her from Lebanon and Amana, from Hermon, the wild haunt of lions; and speaks of her as a garden and as a fountain sealed. A single verse accepts the image in reply.

A verse by the bridegroom follows in the same strain, and once more the bride relates a dream of absence. She calls on the Hebrew ladies to say where her master is, and supposes their answer to tell of his absence. The bridegroom repeats the imagery of Gilead, and prefers her to all his queens and other wives. He tells her how she first appeared beautiful in his eyes when he went down to the valley: "Or ever I was aware, my spirit took me to the chariots of Amminadib," where the veiled beauty was seen (vi. 12). His emblems of herself are borrowed from the fish-pools of Heshbon, and from the tower of Lebanon above Damascus, as well as from the copses of Carmel.

Her answer is contained in a single verse (vii. 10), and the bridegroom again invites her to come with him, through plains and villages, vineyards and gardens of pomegranate. The closing chapter gives the bride's reply, yearning for the bridegroom's presence yet with the refrain —let him not come till he please from the Hebrew land. She pictures her progress from the wilderness to the bridegroom's native land where the apple grows. She proclaims her jealous love in the finest passage in the poem, and speaks of a younger sister not to be compared with her in full-blown beauty. She is herself Solomon's vineyard in Baal Hermon, and once more she calls for his return. "Dweller in gardens, the companions hear thy voice: let me too hear it. Make haste, my love, as a deer or a roe upon the mountains of balm."

There is surely nothing strained in such a reading of the Song. The bride is a Hebrew or Syrian princess from wild regions near Damascus or in Gilead. Amminadib was the name of the king of Ammon in the time of Assurbanipal of Assyria, and according to the Greek version (Cant. vii. 1) it was that of the father of this "prince's daughter." If by Shulamite (vi. 13) we are to understand that she was named from a town called Shulem, we gain little further knowledge, since Shulem is an unknown place. The same passage seems to connect it, according to one reading, with the "dance of Mahanaim" in Gilead. "Return, return, O Shulamite, that we may look on thee. Why will ye gaze on the Shulamite, as at the dance of Mahanaim?" Amminadib may therefore have been an Ammonite prince ruling in Gilead and Bashan, and the Shulamite may have been one of Solomon's Ammonite wives. But, on the other hand, Amminadab (Exod. vi. 23; Ruth iv. 19) was also a Hebrew name meaning "nobly born," and it may have belonged to a Hebrew prince beyond Jordan. Whatever be the race to which the Shulamite princess belonged, there is no epoch in which imagery gathered from all parts of Palestine and of Syria is more natural than in the age of Solomon. The fact that the poem was reverenced by the Jews, in spite of its peculiar nature, points to its antiquity. The word "Paradise" (iv. 13), which occurs in one passage, with other foreign terms,[1] have been thought to point to Persian and to Indian influence. But Solomon's age was one of wide trade, when ivory, apes, and peacocks came by caravan routes (1 Kings x. 22) to the port of Tarshish, or Tarsus, in Asia Minor, and thence to Palestine, bearing Indian names, and when the Queen of Sheba from Yemen herself visited his Court. Cases are known in which words once supposed to be Persian have been traced to the earlier Assyrian; and nothing in the language of the Song of Songs points to the later age of Tyrian trade.

The Book of Proverbs in like manner belongs as a whole to the best age of the Hebrew language. The "Maxims of Ani" in Egypt are the earliest examples of monumental proverbs, and they are older than Solomon's

---

[1] See note, p. 192.

time. The first twenty-four chapters are attributed in the Hebrew text to Solomon, and five are added as "proverbs of Solomon which the men of Hezekiah copied out" (xxv. 1), as though already extant on earlier tablets reduced by them to scrolls. The last two chapters differ in language, and are referred to Agur son of Jakeh of Massah (Prov. xxx. 1; Gen. xxv. 14) on the borders of Edom, and to Lemuel king of Massah (xxxi.) There is an Aramaic tinge in the language of these two chapters, resembling that found in the Edomite Book of Job; but this does not suffice to show late date for the works in question. The word *Bar* for "son"—also found in the second Psalm—is now known to have been used in Syria at least as early as the time of Bar Recab in the eighth century B.C.

When we turn, however, from Proverbs to Ecclesiastes, we find apparently a later language in use, as shown by grammar rather than by words. A Persian word for an "edict" (Eccles. viii. 11) occurs, as in Esther, and many phrases of the later Hebrew are used. The teaching of the Preacher—although Solomon is represented as the hero of the book—seems to argue not a mere disgust with the world, but some acquaintance with a scepticism uncommon in early days, and brought by Greeks to Palestine. "Who knoweth if the spirit of man goeth up, and the spirit of the beast goeth down to earth?" (iii. 21.) The problem of the Preacher is the same as in Job. He sees the vanity of wealth and of power, of sacrifices and of mirth, of deceitful women and of philosophy. He proclaims that God's justice is sure if it is slow: that wisdom and moderation alone bring happiness. "Whatsoever thy hand findeth to do, do it with thy might; for there is no work, nor device, nor knowledge, nor wisdom, in Sheol, whither thou goest" (ix. 10). "Fear God," he concludes, "and keep His commandments; for such is the judgment on man" (xii. 13). The book which so sums up the "whole matter" is not the cynical utterance of a disgusted worldling; it is the wholesome warning against vanity, ambition, and selfishness of one who knew where true wisdom lies. But it belongs to the Wisdom literature, of which another fine example (Ecclesiasticus) is only known to us in Greek, and it seems to be the latest of the great poetic books received into the Hebrew canon.

Such, then, appears to be the history of Hebrew poetry. The early Psalms of David were supplemented with others in the Assyrian age, and others during and after the Captivity. The Book of Job and the Song of Songs preserve to us works not written in Jerusalem, but in Gilead and Edom, and little concerned with Hebrew laws or rites. In Proverbs we find the wisdom of the Hebrews under their kings, with maxims taken from ancient copies, and even from distant tribes. In the Preacher we find repeated the verdict of Job on human life in an age when tyranny and corruption, scepticism and worldliness, were common—perhaps in the last years of the decaying Persian rule.

The testimony of monuments shows us, however, that psalms and songs had been written in Asia long before the time of David which approach in character those attributed to the "sweet singer of Israel." To suppose that most or all of these belong to the later Greek age of the Maccabees, is to ignore the language in which they are written as compared with that in use after Ezra's time.

NOTES TO CHAPTER XI.

Akkadian Hymns.—The bilingual texts which Sir H. Rawlinson published in the 'Cuneiform Inscriptions of Western Asia' have been collected and studied by F. Lenormant in his work called 'Études Accadiennes.' The translations given in the preceding chapter are due to study of the latter work, which gives throughout the cuneiform text in facsimile. They are, however, not always in accordance with Lenormant's results, and are the outcome of independent study by the author. The specimens selected represent the highest attainment of the Akkadian psalmists. They occur side by side with litanies to the "Spirit of Earth" and "Spirit of Heaven," who presided over the countless genii and demons in whom the Akkadians believed. Some of the documents describe charms for exorcising demons, or relate to the mischief done by them. One bilingual is an agreement for renting a house and garden and keeping it in repair. The short Akkadian texts of the earlier kings of Chaldea, such as Urban, Gudea, &c., occur only in that language, as well as the long texts from Tell Loh. The Semitic language first appears in the great inscription of Hammurapaltu about 2100 B.C.

Language of Canticles.—The word Paradise used in this Song (iv. 13) is usually regarded as Aryan—Persian *paradesa*, "a garden"; and several other strange words have been noted. As, however, the Persian is known to have borrowed from the older Assyrian, and Assyrian trade with India goes back to the ninth century B.C. (Obelisk of Shalmaneser II.), such conclusions are at present very doubtful. The use of *shi* for *asher* ("which") found in Canticles, and also in the song of Deborah (Judges v.), is dialectic, but not a mark of date: it is the Assyrian *sa*, used also in the Tell Amarna letters of the fifteenth century B.C.

CHAPTER XII.

THE PERSIAN AGE.

THREE books of the Bible relate the fortunes of the Jews under the Persians—Esther, Ezra, and Nehemiah.

Esther relates the origin of the later festival of Purim, and speaks of the Hebrew wife of Xerxes by her Persian name, "the Star." It uses the Persian words for rulers and satraps; and Purim itself is an Aryan word, connected with the root whence the Latin *fors* is derived. The syntax, no less than the words, of its language, belongs to the later Hebrew, and Persian terms remained in use among the Jews as late as the second century A.D. The author seems to speak of Xerxes (i. 1) as living in a former age, and though he is well informed on Persian customs— such as the establishment of the famous postal service— yet it is difficult to understand how a Jewish maiden could have become the queen of a Persian king, because the law of Persia limited his choice to certain noble Persian families. This discrepancy would be easily understood if the book was written somewhat later. Yet we have no reason to doubt that it contains the true tradition of an Esther whose influence saved her race from persecution—a memory which, in the times of the Maccabees, seems to have still been preserved by the celebration of "the day of Esther," or feast of Purim. The artistic merit of the book, and the vividness of its descriptions, are generally allowed. Nor is it historically improbable that Xerxes should have had a Jewish wife. Cotton is first noticed in the Book of Esther (i. 6), and was, like silk, unknown in Palestine till the later ages of Persian rule.

The Book of Ezra is distinguished as consisting of an introduction, an original memoir, and a final addition, by the use of the third and first persons in its pages. The introduction connects it with Chronicles, repeating the last words of that later history of Israel. It records the return of the Jews in the time of Cyrus, and passes on by the reigns of Darius and of Xerxes down to the age of Artaxerxes. It then includes an Aramaic letter (iv. 8-23) of that reign, to which is apparently added a gloss referring to Darius II. in 425 B.C., which causes great confusion in the history (verse 24). The Aramaic letter of the time of Darius I., when apparently Haggai and Zechariah prophesied (v. 1-vi. 18), is thus out of place, and the later compiler seems to have been little acquainted with Persian history. Another Aramaic decree of Artaxerxes follows (vii. 12-26), and Ezra's own memoir begins at this point in 458 B.C. The sequel by the compiler (x. 1-44) is again in the third person.

This composite work is interesting as showing the official

use of Aramaic in Ezra's age, and as preserving an authentic record in his own words of the return of the Jews to Jerusalem. From what has been said of Chronicles it seems that the additional matter was added to the scattered documents about the end of the fourth century B.C., in the last days of Persian rule.[1]

The Book of Nehemiah presents the same composite character, and its parts are distinguished in the same manner. It begins in 444 B.C. with Nehemiah's own memoir, to which a long addition is made by the later scribe (viii. 1 to xii. 26, 44-47). He refers in the last verse to the "days of Nehemiah" in the past, and inserts (xii. 27-43) another fragment of the original manuscript. He appears to carry down the history to the time of the last Darius, about 332 B.C. (xii. 22), and this agrees with his notice of the high priest Jaddua (verse 11) living in the time of Alexander the Great. The last chapter of this book is Nehemiah's own account of his second visit to Jerusalem in 432 B.C.—according to the usually accepted chronology.

Although the composite character of these books is only clearly seen when they are studied in the original, yet the change from first to third person is sufficient to mark the separation, and the later author in nowise attempts to conceal his personality. The vigour and eloquence of Nehemiah's own writings are in agreement with the

[1] See note, p. 199.

energy of his patriotic nature. The history of Persia is now so well known, through the monumental records of its kings, that we no longer are forced to depend on the Biblical account or on Herodotus alone. The original documents in Ezra and in Nehemiah present by themselves no historical difficulties, but the succession of the kings was perhaps partly forgotten when the later scribe collected and arranged fragments more than a century old.

Of Palestine itself under the Persians very little is known from monuments. The ancient silver shekel coinage belongs, however, to this age, and shows us a character not very different from that used before the Captivity. When we compare these coins—the first struck by the Jews, who in Ezra's age used the Persian Daric—with those struck by the Hasmoneans in the second century B.C., we see that the change in character after the return from exile was very gradual. When these, again, are compared with the character used on tombs in the Herodian age, which are much closer to square Hebrew, the gradual change is still more clearly seen. Hence we may gather that the character of the Hebrew manuscripts, from which Greek translations of Samuel and of later books were made, was that in use about a century before Christ. The Law itself was rendered into Alexandrian Greek as early as 250 B.C., but a later school of translators added the other Jewish books.

The shekel coinage thus appears to show us the character used by Ezra, and it came probably into use in the later Persian time for temple tithes. The coins are dated by the Sabbatic years. They were in value about two shillings and sixpence, whereas the older shekel, used—as a weight—before the Captivity, was three shillings and fourpence value of silver. It weighed 320 grains, against 220 of the later coinage. A Hebrew quarter shekel-weight of about the eighth century B.C. shows us a shekel of 160 grains. But we know that even as late as Roman times the shekel of Galilee was half the Jerusalem shekel. The coinage is almost our only relic of Persian times in Palestine, when the Jews, allowed freedom of worship, lived in submission, till Alexander took Tyre, and Palestine passed without a struggle to the Greeks. Only one work was added to the Hebrew canon after this event, and a consideration of its contents closes our review of Hebrew writings.

The Book of Nehemiah contains valuable notices of Jewish customs, in a time when the few priestly families round Jerusalem observed the Law, which none of the Aramean peasantry followed in the country. New rites and new classes, not mentioned in the Torah, are—as already noted—found established in Ezra's time. New distribution of the tribes in the cities of the south naturally occurred, and such notices confirm the antiquity of earlier books.[1] But the ancient spirit of Hebrew freedom was lost, and later literature does not compare in eloquence with that of the first days of independence.

[1] See note, p. 199.

The bounds of separation from the mixed heathen in Palestine were drawn ever closer, but we have found no reason to think that Ezra tampered with the ancient sacred writings, which became daily more precious to the Jews, or that a spirit of unscrupulous corruption of such texts existed, in a time when Jewish priests once more established the ancient service of Jehovah in Jerusalem.

NOTES TO CHAPTER XII.

Date of Ezra.—The arrival of Ezra in 458 B.C. under Artaxerxes I. (Longimanus) is usually accepted, following Josephus. It has recently been proposed to bring down his history to the time of Artaxerxes II. (Mnemon), following the apparent understanding of the Aramaic chapters, which speak after Cyrus, Darius I., and Xerxes (iv. 5) of Artaxerxes I. (verse 8), and then of Darius II. (Nothus), when the building of the Temple was stopped (iv. 25), then "after these things" of an Artaxerxes (vii. 1) who would be Mnemon. Nehemiah's visits would in this case occur in 385 and 373 B.C., in which case Sanballat might still have been alive under Alexander the Great (333 B.C.), as stated by Josephus.

Topography of the Persian Age.—In Nehemiah xi. 25-36 we have a list of the towns occupied by the children of Judah and Benjamin after the return from Captivity. It includes places which in the earlier topography of Joshua are stated to have belonged to Simeon and to Dan. Thus Moladah, Hazar Shual, Beersheba, Ziklag, and Rimmon were assigned to Simeon (Josh. xix.) Hadid and Neballat (*Hadítheh* and *Bîr Nebala*), with Lod and Ono (*Ludd* and *Kefr 'Âna*), are known to have lain in the territory of Dan, being west of the very carefully described border of Benjamin running from Bethhoron to Kirjath-jearim. This point is worthy of notice, because the topographical chapters of Joshua are assigned by some critics to the age of Ezra, whereas they do not describe the conditions of that age when Benjamin occupied the old country of Dan, and Judah that of Simeon.

CHAPTER XIII.

DANIEL.

THE Book of Daniel has never been reckoned by the Jews as belonging to the library of the earlier prophets. It was always classed with the later works in the canon, and was long doubted before it gained admission.

The book consists of two parts—one written in very late Hebrew, the other in an Aramaic dialect like that in use about the Christian era.[1] Yet, curiously enough, the same critical writers who distinguish two periods in the Books of Ezra and of Nehemiah attribute all Daniel to a single author.

The Hebrew fragments used by the Aramaic compiler seem to have been disconnected, and were arranged by him in a wrong order. The first part refers to the history of Daniel about 605 B.C., and down to the first year of Cyrus (i. 1-21). The dream of Nebuchadnezzar, which follows, appears to have been written on a separate sheet or scroll (ii. 1-3), which was imperfect; and the authority for the Aramaic addition (verses 4-49) is unknown. The prophecy contained in this part refers to the four king-

[1] See note, p. 205.

doms of Assyria, Persia, Greece, and Rome, and to the expectation of an approaching Messianic reign. Another episode of Nebuchadnezzar's time is added, and three Greek names for instruments of music — the *kitharis*, *psalterion*, and *sumphonia*—mark the late period of the Aramaic writer. The Song of the Three Children, with other additions, are found only in the Greek version. In subsequent chapters Nebuchadnezzar is represented to have been followed by Belshazzar, in whose reign the kingdom was taken by Darius the Mede (v. 31)—a king unknown to history; and after him Cyrus the Persian is noticed (vi. 28). It is not impossible that Daniel should have lived in the reign of Nebuchadnezzar and of Cyrus also, but he can hardly have survived from 620 B.C. to the time of the second Darius in 424 B.C.; yet the Hebrew speaks of his prophecy under the son of Xerxes (ix. 1). That there was a Prince Belsaruzur in the time of Cyrus is monumentally known ; but it is certain that Nabonidus was the last Babylonian king, from whom Cyrus took the capital in 536 B.C. There are dated documents in cuneiform to show us that no Darius ruled before Cyrus, and the simplest explanation seems to be that the Aramaic compiler was not familiar with Persian history. He gives us Hebrew prophecies attributed to Daniel, under Cyrus (x. 1) and Darius I. (xi. 1), in 533 and 522 B.C.; but one of his fragments, which he refers to 424 B.C. (ix. 1), precedes both of these. He probably added the words "son of Xerxes" to his text, and confused the second Darius with the successor of Cyrus.

The later Aramaic chapter (vii.) relates the vision of four great beasts, the last of which typifies the rule of Rome. This also contains a clear description of the Messiah, and of the expected end of heathen rule over Israel. When, however, we turn to the concluding Hebrew chapters (viii.-xii), the references carry us only to the time of the Seleucid dynasty (viii. 22), and to the great oppressor Antiochus Epiphanes—or to about 168 B.C. In this chapter the ram is noticed as representing Media and Persia, and the rough goat is "the king of Greece," followed by his four successors—the generals who shared between them the conquests of Alexander the Great.

The famous prophecy of seventy weeks of years (ix.) belongs to the Hebrew part of Daniel. The seventy years of Jeremiah (verse 2) reached from 606 to 536 B.C. (Jer. xxv. 11, 12), and ended with the reign of Cyrus. From the commandment to rebuild Jerusalem (verse 25), which thus seems to be dated in the reign of Cyrus, the prophet reckons seventy weeks of years to be ordained, until the time of a certain Prince a Messiah. If solar years are meant, this would bring us down to the year 46 B.C. The wall of the city was to be built seven weeks from the era, or in 487 B.C.—in the reign of Darius I. In 46 B.C., according to this reckoning, Messiah would be cut off in times of trouble (verse 26), and a few years later the sanctuary would be destroyed. This date coincides with the deposition of the Hasmonean family, and the appointment of the Idumean Antipater as ruler of Palestine. It is, on the other hand, possible that the reference is to an era dating later, when Ezra returned in 458 B.C. to Jerusalem; and seventy weeks of years would bring us to the date of the Crucifixion, in 32 A.D., which is the usual explanation of the prophecy. It is not here intended to enter into such questions, but merely to note that writers who assume the Hebrew to have been written about 170 B.C. can scarcely avoid the further conclusion that the Aramaic chapters must date from a later time, when Roman power was established in the East by the victories of Pompey; and that if the allusion to the destruction of the Anointed Prince be not understood to be prophetical, it is to be regarded as historical, and as referring to the destruction of the native house, superseded by Antipater, the nominee of Julius Cæsar, the Hebrew author fearing that the overthrow of the Temple, and of Jewish religion, would immediately follow.

NOTE TO CHAPTER XIII.

The Language of Daniel.—The Aramaic languages are especially distinguished from Hebrew by the substitution of the letters Daleth, Teth, and Tau for Zain, Tsade, and Shin. Thus the Aramaic words *da*, *Tur*, and *Thor*, answer to the Hebrew *za*, *Tsur*, and *Shor*; and the later Aramaic of the Targums, like the Assyrian, shows these dialectic distinctions. But when we turn to the older language of Syria, which presents many Aramaic features, we find it to agree with the Hebrew in the use of the demonstrative pronoun *za*. If the Aramaic of Daniel were an ancient Syrian dialect, we should expect its phonology to be in accord with the Western Aramaic, whereas it agrees with the Eastern Aramaic of the Book of Ezra and of the later Targums. The pronoun *za* is found at Samala, in the north of Syria, in the eighth century B.C., while on a Jewish tomb of the Herodian age at Jerusalem we find in its place the pronoun *d*. The recovery of the older Aramaic in Syria does not therefore point to the antiquity of the Aramaic language in Daniel.

CHAPTER XIV.

THE TIME OF CHRIST.

The four centuries which passed between the time of Nehemiah and that of the Advent were not fruitful of literature among the Jews. The author of Chronicles lived apparently in the days of the last Darius and of Alexander the Great. The prophecies of Daniel were written down, it would seem, yet later. The memoirs of Ezra and Nehemiah were preserved also by a scribe of the latest Persian times. The Book of Wisdom appears to have been penned about 100 B.C. or later, and Ecclesiasticus a generation earlier. To the same period of Hasmonean rule, under Alexander Jannæus, belongs the valuable history of the great revolt against the Seleucidæ, contained in the 1st Book of Maccabees. But none of these works—written in Greek—found any place in the Hebrew canon. They show us how strong became the Greek influence in Palestine after Alexander's time, and especially after Jewish freedom was re-established for a century by Judas Maccabæus. The Greek philosophy stood side by side with the mixed idolatry of Syrians and Greeks, and it permeated the thoughts of such writers as the Son of Sirach,—the Jewish mind being ever adverse to foreign thought, and contrasting the pure religion of the Prophets of Israel with the vain imaginations of the heathen. But the ideas of rulers were not always in accord with the pious orthodoxy of Pharisees. The Sadducees, who maintained a more primitive belief in Scripture as it stood without the interpretation of later tradition, were indeed the dominant school till Alexander Jannæus died. He himself began to stamp his coins with Greek inscriptions, and called himself "king," departing from the earlier attitude of the Hasmonean house, which claimed only to lead the nation till the expected prophet should come. The palace built in Gilead, about 176 B.C., by a fugitive priest named Hyrcanus, still stands in ruins by the stream of Tyrus. Here, in defiance of the Law, the figures of lions were carved on the cornice—as early Hittites and Syrians also adorned the corners of their palaces; and a few Aramaic letters on the rock give us an alphabet like that of the contemporary Hasmonean coins. No scholar doubts that in this age the law against images existed, and was observed by the Jews; yet here—as on the Galilean synagogues of the second century A.D., when Rabbis of Tiberias were already busy making "a hedge about the Torah"—we find the plain commands of the Pentateuch set at nought. When we compare these facts with the earlier existence of Hebrew seals marked with the orb of the winged sun, or with the yet earlier case of Solomon's lion throne, and carved cherubim in the Temple, we see that the existence of a law against images

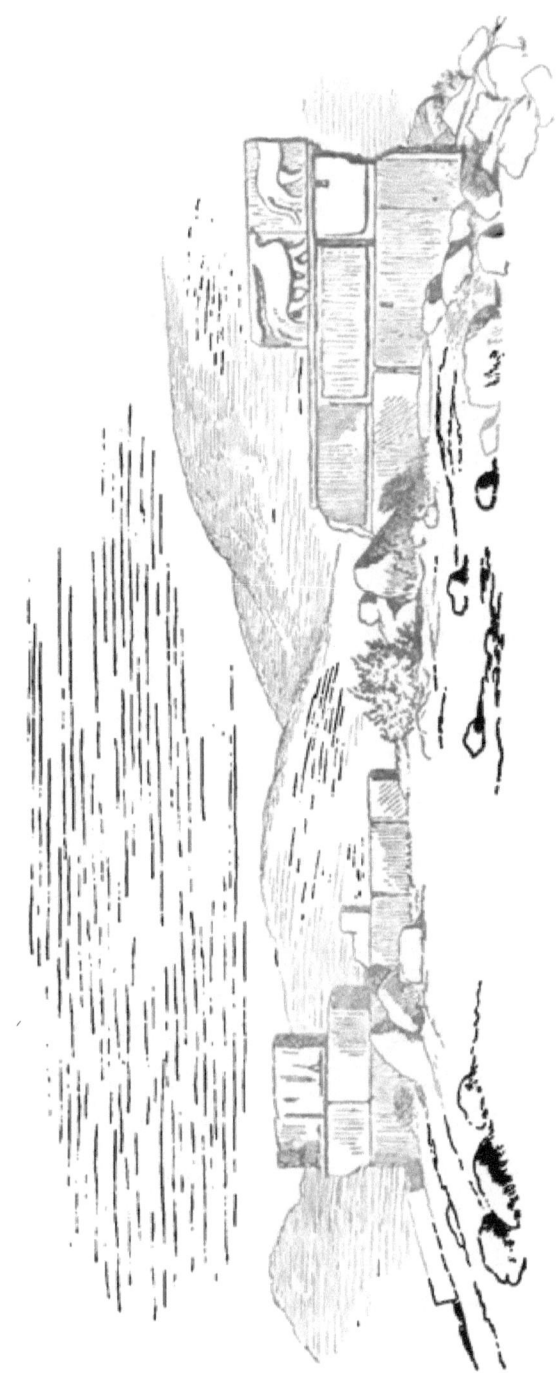

Palace of Hyrcanus.

is not, in any age, refuted by the fact that kings and princes disregarded its precepts. Even priests and Rabbis did so in times when the "Law of Moses" was most sacred in their eyes.

Inscriptions of the Persian and Greek periods, and buildings in Palestine which can be safely referred to that age, are as yet few. We possess the fine silver coins of the Seleucidæ, and the rougher coinage of the Hasmoneans, on which latter the representation of animal life seems to have been forbidden. We also possess the Greco-Phœnician sculptured sarcophagi of Sidon, which seem to be as old as the age of Alexander the Great. We have inscriptions of this same city, and others near Tyre and in Joppa, which belong to the third century B.C., when King Eshmunazar was made the ruler of Sharon by one of the Ptolemies. From his great text we gather that the later Phœnicians continued to worship Baal and Ashtoreth, the old gods of the Amorites; and indeed as late as Roman times the texts found at Beirût show that the same ancient idolatry prevailed, while those of Palmyra carry it on to the third century after Christ.

Architecture was borrowed from the Greeks by Jews and Phœnicians alike. The drafted masonry of the Acropolis, and the cornice decoration, the triglyphs, and frets and honeysuckle patterns of classic Greece, are found in use at the palace of Hyrcanus early in the second century B.C. The ancient form of tomb used by Hebrews and Phœnicians was gradually replaced, about the Christian era, by the Greek tomb, in Cyprus, Phœnicia, and Palestine alike.[1] The Greek language replaced the Persian as the official tongue, and continued to be so used in the East—even to the confines of Persia—down to the seventh century A.D., when it was superseded by Arabic. But it must not be supposed that the Semitic people ceased to use their own language, and their own characters in writing. Abundant evidence exists to show that this was not the case. Not only do Phœnician inscriptions occur in the Greek age, but Palmyrene texts, from the time of Herod down to that of Zenobia, are bilingual, and preserve to us the Syrian character and Syrian language side by side with Greek written in Greek letters.

In the time of Christ three pagan temples were standing in Palestine,—two built at Cæsarea and at Samaria by Herod in honour of Augustus, of which remains exist; and a third at Siah in Bashan, dedicated to the Arab sun-god Aumo, but built in honour of Herod the Great. The last is interesting from its resemblance to the Jerusalem Temple, having a paved court to the east, and a vine carved over its gateway, but differing in so far as the façade was adorned with the image of Aumo. This temple also yields bilingual texts, in Greek and in an Aramaic dialect and character. Thus no less than five alphabets were known in Syria and Palestine in Herod's time—the Phœnician, the Samaritan, the early square Hebrew, the more ornate Palmyrene, and the classic Greek, to which local scripts, with Aramaic dialects, are to be added in Bashan, and at Petra, where Nabathean

---

[1] See note, p. 228.

princes ruled, belonging to the same Idumean race from which Herod also sprang. At Jerusalem, about the Christian era, the priestly family of the Beni Hezir carved a Hebrew text in the square character upon their tomb, which was, however, adorned with a Doric frieze and pillars after the most severe type of Greek architecture.

The outer courts of Herod's Temple at Jerusalem [1] were in like manner Greek in style, with Greek inscriptions. The great ramparts still standing here and at Hebron are built of drafted stones like those of the palace of Hyrcanus in Gilead. The roofs of the Huldah gate—domes supported by primitive imitations of Corinthian pillars—are adorned with classic coffer patterns, among which the Jewish vine meanders. All tombs of the Herodian age, with the later tomb of kings of Adiabene, show us this curious mixture of Greek and native style. Yet in the latter the coffin of Queen Sarah bears an Aramaic text, although the frieze of the façade is semi-Greek in ornament.

Such monuments make clear to us the existence of an Aramaic pagan population side by side with Jews and Greeks. The Greek texts of Bashan are remarkably numerous, and seem to indicate a Greek population in Decapolis side by side with the Arab and Aramean stocks. Greek deities were here adored after the Christian era, together with the earlier Baal, and with gods of Arabia. All such indications are valuable as throwing light on the

[1] See note, p. 223.

Gospels. Thus it is possible that the Gadarene swineherds were Greeks rather than Semitic peasants. To the Phœnician, the Syrian, and the Arab the pig was hardly less unclean than to the Jew. We see also that while Jesus Himself is recorded to have spoken Aramaic, and to have read the Hebrew scriptures, it is by no means unnatural that the Gospel to the Gentiles should have been written in Greek—the official language of the Romans in the East, and the *lingua franca* of the Roman world. Josephus himself so wrote for Romans, and yet earlier the Hasmonean historian, under Alexander Jannæus, wrote his chronicle in the language of the Syrian Court.

Architecture and written texts thus form our surest sources of knowledge as to the conditions prevailing in Palestine in Greek and Roman times. About 150 A.D., when the Mishnah was written at Tiberias in the later Hebrew, Greek and Persian words were used in Hebrew speech. These words, referring to civil law, government, trade, physic, and other matters, bear witness to the close relations which existed between the Jews and their neighbours. Probably the earliest indication of such intercourse is found in the Aramaic chapter in Daniel—already noticed—where Greek names are given to instruments of music. But monumental texts tell us little of the religious and intellectual movements of the age preceding the Advent, and for such questions we must rely on the writings of Philo and of Josephus, and on the earlier apocalyptic books written in the Herodian age.

Josephus himself was a Pharisee of broad views. He

regards the story of Eden as an allegory in which "Moses speaks philosophically." His creed seems to have been affected by the current fashion of attempting to reconcile the ancient Scriptures with the Greek philosophy of Athens and of Alexandria — a fashion which is visible in the Book of Wisdom, and which led to Philo's attempt to reconcile the Torah with the Platonic theory of the Logos and Anastasis. Such views, no doubt as early as the time of Alexander Jannæus, found favour with the Hellenists, whose admiration of all Greek culture conflicted with the sterner precepts of the Law. Jewish opinion was thus naturally divided between the schools of the Sadducees, who found in the Torah no teaching of resurrection; of the Pharisees, whose traditions often show marks of Persian influence; and of the Hellenists, whose view of the future was based on Plato.

But other influences were at work in Hasmonean and Herodian times. The Stoics had appeared in Syria, and their doctrines were accepted by Athenians and Romans. Yet earlier (according to Josephus, Apion, i. 22) an Indian colony of hermits seems to have been established in Syria, and bore the name of "Sugar-cane" people—the name of the family of Buddha. There seems, therefore, to be reason for supposing that Buddhist missionaries, who began to spread from the kingdom of Asoka about 250 B.C., had already penetrated to the Phœnician shores before the time of Christ. That Asoka knew the names of the Greek rulers of the West we learn from his own inscriptions; and the same Ptolemy for whom the Law was rendered into Greek is said to have collected Buddhist books in his library. The hermits had long practised self-mortification in India, and had been met in Persia by Alexander the Great—one even being recorded to have come to Greece. In the second century A.D. Buddhists were found in Alexandria, and the legend of Buddha was known to St Jerome. It is not impossible, therefore, that the appearance of monastic sects in Palestine as early as the Hasmonean age, and in Egypt before the time of Philo, may yet be traceable to Buddhist influence. There is much in the description of the Essenes by Josephus that recalls the rules of the Buddhist *Sangha* or religious society. The existence of monasteries, the simplicity of dress, the common fund, the wanderings from place to place, are characteristic both of Buddhist missionaries and of the Essenes. The Egyptian Therapeutæ had the same customs as described by Philo. But the Essenes were not Indians, nor were they Buddhists only. They observed Hebrew rites, and read Hebrew Scriptures, although they abandoned sacrifices, and are said to have held peculiar tenets of their own. The resemblance between the Essenes and the early Christians has often been pointed out; but the celibacy of this Jewish sect was contrary to the plain teaching of Jesus concerning marriage, and to the practice of his wedded disciples.

Another feature of the age preceding Christ was the widespread expectation of a future Saviour of the world. In Persia it was already believed that Zoroaster would return in the last days together with the risen righteous,—born of a virgin mother in an eastern lake, he was expected to conquer the world and re-establish the creed of Ormuzd. In India the expectation of a World-king, and of a future Buddha—also virgin-born—was already ancient. Even in Virgil we find an echo of the same hope in the days of Augustus, due perhaps to the influence of the earlier so-called Sibylline oracles, penned in Greek hexameters by a Jewish poet of Alexandria before the Christian era.[1] In the Hebrew prophets we read of a kingdom of God, a judgment-day, and a future king of David's house; but in the Greek age the author of the 1st Book of Maccabees speaks only of an expected prophet. The Prince Messiah first appears distinctly in the Hebrew of Daniel, but during the Herodian age many works existed in which the Messianic kingdom was fully described. The strange Book of Enoch, with its description of an inferno like that of Dante, is probably older than the Christian era. The so-called Psalms of Solomon belong to the Herodian age. The 3d Book of Esdras was known to Josephus; the Book of Baruch existed perhaps in 100 B.C. Such comparisons show us that not only the Jews in Herod's time expected a Messiah, but that the Gentiles also looked forward to a Saviour of the world. The first Gospel tells us that wise men from Persia came to seek that Saviour in the rocky stable at Bethlehem.

The Roman peace descended on a war-worn world in

---

[1] See Drummond's 'Jewish Messiah.'

the time of Augustus: the Idumean tyrant Herod died in the year of the Advent, and was buried in the great round palace at Herodium, which still stands facing Bethlehem: ten years later Archelaus was deposed in 6 A.D., and Cyrenius became governor of Palestine. During the lifetime of Jesus, Coponius, Marcus Ambivius, Annius Rufus, and Valerius Gratus succeeded each other as procurators of Judea, before the placeman Pontius Pilate became the unworthy and unsuccessful representative of Tiberius in Jerusalem in 25 A.D. His recall was ordered by the Emperor in 36 A.D., probably five years after the Crucifixion. The coins of Augustus and Tiberius replaced the native coinage of Herod and his sons. The tribute "penny" rendered to Cæsar was stamped with the image of the master of the world, and other coins were issued by the procurators. Whether the Temple tithes were paid in ancient silver shekels we do not know from any existing coinage, but the statement of the Mishnah concerning the new shekels of the sanctuary seems to refer to the Roman age. Nothing is more remarkable in the Gospels than the scarcity of reference to Roman affairs. The names of Cyrenius and Pontius Pilate occur, with notice of the Herodian party, bent on re-establishing the Idumean family, which, under Agrippa, they succeeded in doing after the time of Christ. But the scene of the ministry is laid in regions remote from the central capitals at Cæsarea, Sepphoris, or Samaria, and only in the last episode of the entry to Jerusalem does the narrative bring before us the Roman governor, with the crafty Herodian intriguer.

The central part of Palestine in this age—between Shechem and Galilee—was no longer a sacred land to the Jew. The law of the seventh year, which was not binding in Syria, was no doubt observed in Samaria; but the schism which dated from the days of Ezra was already complete. It was based on the ancient jealousy of Joseph and of Judah, which we trace back to the times of Joshua and of David. It was rendered more bitter by the idolatry of Hamathite and Assyrian colonists, who worshipped Jehovah with other gods after 721 B.C. in Shechem. The Hebrew priestly family which observed the Law on Gerizim, and clung to the earliest of Hebrew shrines where Joseph's and Eleasar's tombs were shown beneath the mountain, with Jacob's well, had been estranged already when Nehemiah rebuilt the walls of Jerusalem and Ezra re-established its Temple service. But the people whom they led were of mixed blood—Cutheans from beyond the Euphrates, and Syrians from the north; and separation from the heathen was not more strictly enforced from Ezra's time than separation from the priests of Samaria. The Pharisees especially were bitter against them, and John Hyrcanus destroyed their temple. Yet in some respects the Law was observed more exactly in Shechem than in Jerusalem during the Herodian age. The Passover on Gerizim was eaten in haste with loins girt. At Jerusalem, as we learn both from the Gospels and from the Mishnah, it was eaten by the Jews seated at ease (as in our own times); and the sacramental cup of wine, to which both the Gospels and the Mishnah refer, formed no part of the original rite as described in the Torah, although the custom (still extant) dates back to the Christian era.

It is not here proposed to enter at length into literary questions regarding the Gospels. Critical opinion has of late undergone a change in this question quite as remarkable as the change which has occurred in criticism of the Pentateuch. But in the case of the New Testament the critical view has receded, and the dates for the Gospels now proposed differ by only about thirty years from those deduced from the testimony of Papias (130 A.D.), as preserved by Eusebius. Towards the close of the second Christian century the four Gospels of the Muratorian canon bore the same names still known to us, and were received as scripture by Christian writers. The Epistle of Barnabas so quotes the Gospel of Matthew, and is dated not later than 100 A.D. The Gospels bear in two cases the names of disciples of the second generation; and even those "according to Matthew" and "according to John" were not of necessity penned by those apostles. The first Gospel was that of the Church in Palestine, and is the most strictly Jewish in tone. The third is believed to be the Gospel of the Church of Antioch, and the second the Gospel of the Church of Rome. Irenæus believed that the fourth Gospel was the latest, and represented that of the Church of Ephesus. The ancient Hebrew Gospel, of which Jerome speaks, has never been recovered. It may be represented by that common element which is found in the three first Gospels; and in this respect the Gospel of Mark seems most closely to approach it. But the extant Gospels are not translations from Hebrew or from Aramaic. They were written in Greek, except perhaps the first, but written by Hebrews, who have at times preserved their native idiom when writing in the common tongue of the Roman world. The third Gospel is remarkable for its tolerance of the Gentiles; and the fourth employs phrases of the current Platonic philosophy of Athens, Ephesus, and Alexandria. Accounts not seemingly known to every Church distinguish Matthew, Luke, and John from Mark, and from each other; and unless it should hereafter be shown that Cyrenius was ruling in Syria in the time of Herod the Great,[1] and that a census was made of the Roman world other than those of Augustus mentioned in the great Angora inscription, it would seem — according to our present information — that the Church in Palestine and the Church in Antioch differed, by ten years, in the date to which they referred the Nativity. Christian opinion differed much in the time of Irenæus as to the length of the Saviour's life, but all the Gospels place the Crucifixion in the time of Pontius Pilate.

There were, no doubt, many other early accounts of the history of Jesus which have not been preserved. To such the fourth Gospel and the third alike refer. The early fathers speak of a "Gospel of the Egyptians" and of a "Gospel of the Hebrews," which, from the extracts

[1] See note, p. 229.

quoted, differed from those received by all the Churches. They seem to have belonged to early Gnostic sects, and were succeeded in the fourth and fifth centuries by others still well known. That which distinguishes the four Gospels from such heretical books is the preservation of all that we most love and reverence in their pages. We look in vain in Apocryphal Gospels, of Peter or of James, for the parables of the Sower, of the Prodigal Son, of the Good Samaritan, for the Sermon on the Mount, or for that "sweet story of old" of Jesus and little children. They are full of marvels—the bowing palm and the Egyptian dragon—with malevolent miracles of the infant Christ; they often remind us of the legend of Buddha; and the Gnostics are known to have welded into one chaotic mixture the Christian teaching, the Persian legends, the Eleusinian mysteries, and the Buddhist beliefs. The reason why the four Gospels became so generally accepted, in Italy, in Alexandria, at Carthage, in Palestine, and in Asia Minor, is not hard to find when they are compared with such works of the Gnostics.

Literary discoveries of the highest value have recently widened our knowledge of the early Christian age. The recovery of the Epistle of Clement (in Turkey) and of that of Barnabas (preserved with the Gospels in the fourth century at Sinai) was followed by that of the "Teaching of the Apostles," which seems to give us the belief of Ebionite Christians at Pella and Kokaba in Bashan, where—according to tradition—the brethren of Jesus lived after the fall of Jerusalem. To the Ebionites He was but a prophet and servant of God. The sacred Supper was but a symbol of the approaching time in which the scattered Church should be gathered "into one loaf": the prayer of the cup relates only to the truth and immortality revealed by "Thy servant Jesus"; and the prophets still ranked with apostles, bishops, teachers, and deacons among those who yet expected immediately a second Advent. It is curious that the presbyter or priest is not mentioned in this ancient work of the second Christian century; for the title—like that of bishop—was ancient, and was of civil origin. It belonged to the political system of the Roman world; and pagan presbyters are noticed, as well as pagan bishops, in the texts of Bashan and of Asia Minor. The Ebionites are known to have accepted a Gospel which did not include the first chapters of Matthew. They survived in Bashan until the power of the Greek Church was established, when they were persecuted for heresy. The works of Justin Martyr show us, however, that about a century after the Crucifixion the "Memoirs of the Apostles" were read in the gatherings of Syrian Christians on the "Lord's day"—the first day of the week—side by side with Hebrew scriptures, and that the simplicity of Christianity allowed, in that early time, of extemporary prayers long before any ritual had grown up in any of the Churches. We have the testimony of Pliny to the innocent life of the early Christians in Pontus; and we have allusions to John the Baptist, to Jesus Himself, and to James, in Josephus, which there is no reason to regard as forged interpolations. But we have no account in early times of one united Church. The Bishop of Rome was not acknowledged as the head of all Churches in the days of Irenæus or of Chrysostom, or indeed in any age after the great schism between Greeks and Romans. The early Fathers—excepting Clement—were chiefly Syrians and dwellers in Africa. The liturgies of the Churches differed from the first; and that of Gaul was very different from that of Jerusalem when St Sylvia visited Palestine in the fourth century A.D.

Such discoveries have thrown more light on Christian history than any inscriptions yet recovered. The catacombs of Rome, and a few texts in Palestine and Asia Minor, are as yet our only monumental sources of knowledge. The Christians were persecuted and afraid to own their faith. Till Constantine's time they never used the cross upon their brief mortuary texts. The fish (*ichthus*), symbolising "Jesus Christ the Son of God," was their most daring emblem, and is recommended by Clement of Alexandria as a sign on Christian signets. The letters X.M.G.—for "Christ born of Mary"—are found in Syria on Christian inscriptions of the early centuries before the Council of Nicæa; but as a rule it is almost impossible to distinguish Christians from worshippers of Mithra and Serapis, or of other heathen gods, in the first ages of the Church.

The ancient pagan systems had in these ages become mingled together. The worship of Baal survived in Syria with that of Apollo, and hermits stood on pillars at the great Carchemish temple, as they stood much earlier in India, and stood again, later, in Syria and on the banks of Jordan, when the Stylites copied the heathen custom. In Rome itself the Madonna-like worship of Isis and her babe, and the mysteries of Mithra, including the sacred *haoma* drink and the cake—regarded by the Fathers as a parody of the Christian rite—had almost superseded the Roman native rites of Jupiter. The dogma of transubstantiation was part of the Mithra worship, which Pompey's soldiers had brought from Persia before the Christian era. But as yet no cardinals of a Roman Church had donned the garb of the Flamens: no Pope had called himself Pontifex Maximus—successor of the pagan high priest of Rome, or "Vicar of Christ"—a term which Tertullian uses of the Holy Ghost. The pagan systems long opposed the silent growth of Christian belief; but when defeated and neglected, paganism found its revenge, in Italy, in the corruption of the simplicity of Christ.

Exploration of Palestine has done much to establish the genuineness of the fourth Gospel, by showing its accuracy in matters of geography. Not only does its author quote the Hebrew Scriptures as opposed to the Greek variations, but it is clear that the topography of all parts of Palestine was known to him when he wrote. Christian tradition from Constantine's time placed the scene of the baptism on Jordan near Jericho—a site not to be reconciled with the distance from Beth-Abarah, "house of the ford" (where the baptism is said in the fourth Gospel to have occurred), to Cana in Galilee, which

THE SITE OF CALVARY.

was but a day's journey distant. The name Abarah is, however, now known to apply to a ford much farther north, and near to the vicinity of Cana. The site of Enon near Salem is also found east of Shechem, and Sychar by Jacob's well at 'Askar (the Samaritan Ischar), immediately east of Shechem. To the fourth Gospel we owe the only clear notices of the position of Calvary, near the gardens " nigh unto the city." The site which Constantine chose—the hill of Akra—has been shown, by the recovery of the second wall, to have lain not near but within the city in the time of Christ. Josephus speaks of gardens, in 70 A.D., north of Jerusalem; and it is here, upon a rounded knoll, that Jewish tradition still preserves the site of that " House of Stoning " noticed in the Mishnah, where the criminal executed by order of the Sanhedrin used to be crucified after stoning. We can hardly doubt that the site so pointed out is the real place of execution, and the Calvary which—like the knoll in question—was near the city but visible from " afar off." When Godfrey of Bouillon set up his engines against the city, striving to win the Holy Sepulchre, his mailed feet must often have pressed upon the very spot where in truth Christ had suffered, and the blood of men slaughtered in the cause of Christian dogma deluged the great cathedral of the holy tomb; but the true Calvary was not so defiled by fanatics, who passed it by unnoticed and unknown.

This slight sketch of Bible history, as viewed in the light of modern discovery, must here close. The only object set before the reader is the discovery of truth concerning the history of the Hebrews. Cases in which literary criticism leads to results supported by monumental records have been duly noticed, but these belong to the later books of the Bible. The second author in Isaiah, the composite character of the Books of Ezra and Nehemiah, the late date of Chronicles and Daniel, and probably of Esther, have been set forth. The confusion caused by hasty assumption in the cases of the Exodus and of Ahab of Sirbai, have also been charged against the early students of monumental texts. The antiquity of the Pentateuch has been advocated solely on historic and monumental evidence, although the latest theory of its nature has been incidentally explained to lead to untenable results. The unity of Joshua, Judges, Samuel, Job, and Solomon's Song, and the antiquity of the "prayers of David the son of Jesse," have been argued by reference to yet older writings preserved for us in Assyria, and by explanation of the more recent results of exploration, as bearing on geography in Palestine — a question which also affects our study of the "Gospel after John." The existence of a collection of ancient tablets, transcribed later on rolls in alphabetic character, has been shown to explain many difficulties in the literary structure of the Torah. It is only by using every means at our command that we can hope at length to read the Bible aright. Valuable as is internal study of its contents, the testimony of independent accounts is yet more conclusive. Nor must we ever forget that the Hebrews were an oriental people, whose thoughts and beliefs and customs are best studied by the light of oriental character in our own times. Theories of the scholar's chamber, which are natural to those who have never lived in the East, often betray a modern cast of thought, which has little in common with the facts of oriental antiquity. The wind of the desert blows over the pages of Job, and the Song of Solomon pictures the rocks and woods of Gilead. The voice of Moses in the wilderness echoes in the Law; and the imagination of captive priests in Babylon can never have given birth to the archaic enactments of the Torah. It is the voice of the Hebrews in times of power and freedom which we still hear in stories of Samuel or of Joseph, which no writer of to-day can rival in their simplicity and tender human interest and beauty.

NOTES TO CHAPTER XIV.

Hebrew and Greek Tombs.—The ancient form of Hebrew and Phœnician tomb was a square rock-cut chamber, with tunnels for the bodies at the sides. The corpses lay with their feet towards the chamber, and the tunnel was closed by a slab. About the Christian era (in the tombs of the kings of Adiabene and that of the Bene Hezir priests at Jerusalem) we find this form of tomb gradually replaced by one which had rock-cut sarcophagi, under arches so placed at the sides of the chamber that the body lay parallel with the wall. The sarcophagus was covered over with slabs, having an arched recess above. The door of the tomb was often closed by a cylindrical stone rolling on its edge. In some tombs the outer or older chambers are Hebrew, while the inner have this later Greek arrangement, which continued to be used by Christians in Palestine at least as late as the ninth century A.D. The tomb described in the Gospels, with a rolling-stone and a sarcophagus so placed that an angel could be seated at the head and another at the foot of the body (John xx. 12), was clearly a Greek tomb; but the change was only just occurring about the time of Christ.

Inscriptions of Herod's Temple.—The Greek prohibitory text, found by M. Clermont Ganneau, and which was one of those set up to divide the outer court of Gentiles from the inner court of Israel, is written in fine classic capitals, which are evidence of the Greek character used in the time of Christ. At the base of the outer wall of the Temple Sir C. Warren, however, discovered Semitic letters, on the stones near the south-east corner, which the late Dr E. Deutsch hastily assumed to be of the age of Solomon. We are now able to compare them with specimens of various ages, from the ninth to the second century B.C., and there can be little doubt that these mason's marks could more properly be assigned to the Herodian period. The character of the masonry on which they occur is distinctively Greek, and we have no example of such drafted masonry before the Greek age. The earliest known example belongs to the Acropolis at Athens. In Palestine it is found in the palace of Hyrcanus (176 B.C.), and it was used later by Romans, Byzantines, and Crusaders. Wherever it occurs in Phœnicia it is, as a rule, accompanied by Greek details of architectural ornamentation. It is unknown as a Hebrew finish to masonry.

Cyrenius.—The passage (Luke ii. 1-3) which speaks of the taxing under Augustus, when "Cyrenius was governor of Syria," appears clearly to refer to a period after the death of Herod the Great. P. Sulpicius Quirinus was Legate of Syria from 5 A.D., and was preceded by P. Quintilius Varus (3 B.C. to 5 A.D.), and by C. Sentius Saturninus (7 B.C. to 3 B.C.) The history of Quirinus has been studied, and it is not known where he may have been about 4 or 3 B.C., but he was not then the Legate of Syria. These verses may have been added as a gloss, and the "taxing" of Joseph (verse 4) thus connected with the census of a later period, by a writer who had not before him the second chapter of Matthew, which places the Nativity in the "days of Herod the king."

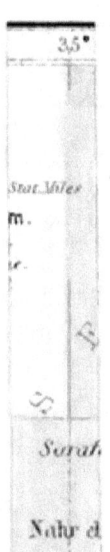

INDEX.

Aaron, 96.
Abiri (Hebrews), 36, 41, 103.
African languages, 9, 15.
Ahab, 149.
Ahmes, 42.
Akkadian language, 13, 20, 21, 31.
Akkadians, 20, 29, 173-177, 192.
Alphabets, 61, 74, 211.
Amenophis, 30, 36, 39, 40, 41.
American languages, 9, 14, 17.
Amminadib, 186, 188.
Amorites, 25, 29, 33, 40, 45, 101, 103, 118, 121.
Amraphel, 23, 28, 33.
Antiquity of man, 7.
Apes, 77, 163.
Aphek, 136.
Apophis, 31.
Arabs, 16, 25, 27, 211, 213.
Aramaic language, 25, 30, 33, 54, 56, 194, 201, 205, 212.
Archaisms in Pentateuch, 74.
Architecture, 210, 212.
Arioch, 23, 28.
Arkah, 27, 33.
Arvad, 27, 32, 33, 40, 121, 155.
Asaph Psalms, 183.
Ascalon, 40, 41, 43, 110.
Asherah, 121.
Ashkenaz, 24.
Assur-bani-pal, 155, 174.
Assur Nirari, 152.
Assyrians, 25, 33, 96, 99, 118, 147, 152.

Australian language, 9, 14.

Babylon, 25, 26, 29, 77, 112, 118, 147, 154, 155.
Babylonian Canon, 29, 34.
    ,,   Flood Story, 16.
Batrun, 28, 40.
Beersheba, 28.
Belshazzar, 202.
Bethabara, 224.
Bethel, 85, 101.
Book of Covenant, 92.
    ,,   Jasher, 108, 143.
    ,,   Odes, 143.
    ,,   Wars of Jehovah, 98.
Buddhists, 17, 214.

Calvary, 225.
Canaanites, 25, 27, 33, 39, 78, 98, 101, 117.
Canon, Babylonian, 29, 34.
    ,,   Eponym, 159.
Carchemish, 28, 39, 151, 224.
Cassites, 21.
Celts, 24.
Central shrine, 81, 123, 129.
Chaldea, 25.
Chinese language, 9, 14.
Chronolgy, 148, 158-162, 194, 195, 201.
Cimmerians, 24.
Cities taken by Thothmes III., 33, 110.
Civilisation, 19, 53, 67, 76.
Coins, 196, 210.

232 INDEX.

Comparison of languages, 13.
Creation tablet, 175.
Critical views, 81-90, 131-137, 184, 219.
Cross, 223.
Cubit, 158.
Curse of Gudea, 174.
Cushites, 21, 25.
Cypriote syllabary, 75.
Cyrenius, 217, 220, 229.

Damascus, 27, 32, 39, 40, 150, 152, 153.
Dan, 27, 28, 80.
Danai (Greeks), 24, 32.
Dardani, 32.
Date of Exodus, 35.
  " Ezra, 199.
Dates (see Chronology).
  " Egyptian, 51.
Deuteronomy, 90, 109, 112.
Dothan, 27, 32.
Dusratta, 31, 39, 71, 77, 112.

Ebionites, 222.
Edom, 41, 45, 50, 168, 178.
Egyptian language, 9, 15, 19.
Egyptians, 19, 38-41, 51, 106, 119-121, 149, 154.
Elam, 20, 25.
Elephants, 77.
Elishah, 24, 77.
Ellasar, 29.
Elohim, 64, 88, 129, 182.
Eponym lists, 159.
Eriaku, 23, 34.
Esarhaddon, 155.
Essenes, 215.
Exodus, 35.

Fauna of Pentateuch, 69.
Finnic languages, 13.
Flood, 10.

Gaza, 25, 27, 39, 43, 110.
Gebal, 28, 40, 77, 110, 152, 155.
Genesis, 1, 175.
Geography, 26, 43, 107, 114, 120, 141, 199.
Gerar, 27, 33.
Gezer, 33, 40.
Gihon, 157, 158.
Greek words, 202.
Greeks, 24, 62, 207, 212, 228.

Ham, 25.
Ham (land), 29, 33.
Hamath, 27, 75, 152.
Hammurapaltu, 23, 29.
Haran, 27, 28, 39.
Hebrew language, 54, 205.
Hebrews (see Abiri).
Hebron, 30, 39, 103, 106.
Herod, 211, 217.
Hieroglyphics, 19, 60, 74, 75.
Hittites, 25, 27, 29, 39, 41, 62, 74, 75, 99, 102, 119, 121, 125.
Hobah, 29, 33.
Home of man, 8.
  " Semitic, 22.
Hyksos, 25, 31, 38.
Hyrcanus, palace of, 208.

Ideograms, 64, 76.
Invasions of Palestine, 24, 32, 80, 118, 120.
Ionians, 24, 25, 26, 74, 160.

Japhet, 24.
Jehovah, 65, 71, 72, 73, 78, 88, 129, 182.
Jerusalem, 27, 40, 101, 109, 120, 154.
Joppa, 33, 110, 122, 154.
Jordan, passage of, 108.

Kadesh Barnea, 44, 45, 46, 52, 89.
  " of Hagar, 46, 52.
  " on Orontes, 33, 39, 119, 128, 139, 142.
Keratiya, 139.
Kings, Hebrew, 80, 91, 98, 99.

Lachish, 30, 40, 105.
Language, 9, 13, 53-60, 74, 87, 107, 117, 144, 169, 188, 189, 192, 205, 211, 213.
Laws, ancient, 99, 112.
Leku, 32.
Levites, 82, 83, 96, 123, 129, 146.
Leviticus, 92.
Lydda, 33, 199.
Lydians, 25.

Manetho, 35, 51.
Manuscripts, 87, 128, 160, 196.
Massah, 189.
Matiene, 31, 77.
Medes, 24.
Megiddo, 32, 39, 107, 122.

INDEX.   233

Merodach Baladan, 154, **166**.
Messiah, 165, 203, 216.
Mineptah, 32, 41, 120, 125.
Minyans, 22, 23, 25, 31, 38.
Mitani (Matiene), 31, 77.
Moab, 46, 50, 56, 103, 147.
Moabite Stone, 55, 71, 111, **149**, 160.
Mongols, 9, 10, 20.
Mouth names, 144.
Moschi, 24.

Nabonidus, 155, 202.
Natural history, 30, 69.
Nebuchadnezzar, 155, 169, **202**.
Necho, 155.
Nethinim, 85, 98.
Nineveh, 25, 154, 155, 167.
Numerals in Bible, 44, 51, 128, 159.

Palmyra, 146, 150.
Paradise, 188, 192.
Parallel passages, 86, 93, 94.
Passover, 218.
Pentateuch, 57-67, 79-99.
Persian words, 57, 188, 189, 213.
Persians, 193, 196.
Petra, 27, 29, 46, 52, 178.
Philistines, 25, 27, 32, 102, 110, 117, 120, 121, 147.
Phœnicians, 28, 39, 40, 62, 151.
Poetry, 173-192.
Polynesian languages, 10, 14.
Priests (David's sons), 130.
Priests' Code, 89.
Prophets, 84, 97, 109, 146, 147, 165.
Psalms, Akkadian, 175, 192.
    ,, Hebrew, 181.
Purim, 193.
Pyramids, 23.

Races of Genesis, 24.
Rameses (city), 28, 35.
Rameses II., 41, 99, 119, 125.
    ,, III., 32, 120.
    ,, XVI., 96.
Red Sea, 44, 45.
Rephaim, 171.
Rimmon Nirari, 151, 166.
Romans, 217.
Roots of language, 16.
Route of Exodus, 44.

Rude stone **monuments**, 78.

Samala, 152.
Samaria, 27, 85, **110**, **159**.
Samaritans, 218.
Saul, 132.
Semitic home, 22, **29**.
    ,, languages, **9**, 15, 53, 74.
Sennacherib, 153.
Seti I., 41, 118, 124.
Shairdana, 32.
Shalmaneser II., **151**.
Shasu, 41.
Sheba, 26.
Shechem, 39, 81, 101, 109, 110.
Shekels, 197.
Shem, 25.
Sheol, 166, 171.
Shinar, 29, 33.
Shishak, 36, 96, 149.
Shulamite, 187.
Siamese languages, 9.
Sidon, 27, 33, 40, 151, 210.
Siloam text, 54, 61, 147, 156, 158.
Sinai, 20, 26, 29, 39, 41, 42, 44, 48.
Sisera, 119.
Solomon, 36, 102.
Song of Jacob, 109.
    ,, Songs, 183-188.
Spirits of earth and heaven, 23.
Stations in the desert, 43-49.
Stone stages, 8.
Style, 88.
Succoth, 44.
Sychar, 225.
Symbols (Christian), 223.

Tablets, 62, 66, 67, 91, 98.
Tadukhepa, 30, 39, 77.
Tarshish, 24, 150, 162.
"Teaching of the Apostles," 221.
Teie, 30, 40.
Tell Amarna tablets, 32, **41**, 71, 77, 98, 103, 118.
Temple, 138, 139, 212, 223.
Teraphim, 130.
Thebes, 168.
Thothmes III., 29, 32, 38, 43, 51.
Tiglath Pileser III., 111, 152, 153.
Tin, 162, 163.
Tirhakah, 153, 167.
Tirzah, 27, 85, 110.

Q

Tithes, 99, 128.
Togarmah, 24.
Tombs, 228.
Torah or Law, 79-99, 208.
Transcribing the Law, 93, 95.
Tunep (Tennib), 33, 40, 119.
Tuplai, 24.
Turkish languages, 13.
Twelve Tribes, 111, 114, 115, 116, 120.
Tyre, 33, 40, 212, 151, 152, 155, 170.

Unicorn, 69.
Unity of Pentateuch, 87.
Unknown prophet, 167.
Ur, 28.

Versions of Old Testament, 87, 107, 127, 159, 169, 202.

War-song, 174.
Writing, 60-64.
Writings of Moses, 91, 98.
Written Law, 83.

Zemar (Semyra), 27, 33.
Ziggurs (pyramids), 23.

THE END.

PRINTED BY WILLIAM BLACKWOOD AND SONS.

www.ingramcontent.com/pod-product-compliance
Lightning Source LLC
Chambersburg PA
CBHW031738230426
43669CB00007B/394